The Tale of Bolli Bollason

Original Text, Translations, and Word Lists

Translated by
Matthew Leigh Embleton

Copyright ©2025 Matthew Leigh Embleton. All rights reserved.

The Tale of Bolli Bollason

The Tale of Bolli Bollason (*Old Norse*)..4
Word List *(Old Norse to English)*..40
Word List *(English to Old Norse)* 57
The Tale of Bolli Bollason (*Old Icelandic*) 70
Word List *(Old Icelandic to English)*..105
Word List *(English to Old Icelandic)*..122
A Word Comparison of Old Norse and Old Icelandic Words 136

Cover: Old Norse text over an outline of Iceland. Author's design.

The original Old Norse and Old Icelandic texts are in the public domain.
These translations ©2022 Matthew Leigh Embleton
©2025 Matthew Leigh Embleton (This Edition)

Acknowledgments

I have long been fascinated by languages and history, and I am very grateful to the special people in my life who have supported and encouraged me in my work. Thank you for believing in me. You know who you are.

Introduction

Old Norse is a North Germanic language spoken by inhabitants of Scandinavia from about the 7th to the 15th centuries. Old Icelandic is a variety of Old West Norse that emerged during the Norse settlement of Iceland in the second half of the 9th century. The rich tradition of Icelandic literature survived by oral tradition over several centuries before being written down in the 13th Century. The Tale of Bolli Bollason (*Bolla þáttr Bollasonar*) is one of the many Tales of Icelanders or *Íslendingaþættir*. The word '*þáttr*' (plural: '*þættir*') translates as a strand of rope or a yarn, comparable to the word 'yarn' in English sometimes used to refer to a story.

This book contains:
- The Tale of Bolli Bollason (*Bolla þáttr Bollasonar*) (Old Norse Version)
- An Old Norse to English Word List
- An English to Old Norse Word List
- The Tale of Bolli Bollason (*Bolla þáttr Bollasonar*) (Old Icelandic Version)
- An Old Icelandic to English Word List
- An English to Old Icelandic Word List
- A Word Comparison of Old Norse and Old Icelandic words

The texts are presented in their original form, with a literal word-for-word line-by-line translation, and a Modern English translation, all side-by-side. In this way, it is possible to see and feel how the worked and how it has evolved. This book is designed to be of use and interest to anyone with a passion for the Old Norse or Old Icelandic language, Norse history, or languages and history in general.

The Tale of Bolli Bollason (*Old Norse*)

Old Norse	Literal	English
1	**1**	**1**
Í þann tíma, er Bolli Bollason bjó í Tungu ok nú var áðr frá sagt, þá bjó norðr í Skagafirði á Miklabæ Arnórr kerlingarnef, sonr Bjarnar Þórðarsonar frá Höfða.	At the time, that Bolli Bollason lived at Tunga also now was earlier from told, then lived north in Skagafjord in Miklabaer Arnor Crone's-Nose, son-of Bjarni Son-of-Thord from Hofdi.	At the same time that Bolli Bollason lived at Tunga, as was spoken of earlier, Arnor Crone's-Nose lived north at Skagafjord in Miklabaer, he was the son of Bjarni Thordarson from Hofdi.
Þórðr hét maðr, er bjó á Marbæli.	Thord named a-man, who lived at Marbaeli.	There was a man named Thord who lived at Marbaeli.
Guðrún hét kona hans.	Gudrun named wife his.	His wife was named Gudrun.
Þau váru vel at sér ok höfðu gnótt fjár.	They were well of themselves and had an-abundance of-wealth.	They were fine people and had an abundance of wealth.
Sonr þeira hét Óláfr, ok var hann ungr at aldri ok allra manna efniligastr.	Son theirs named Olaf, and was he young in age and of-all men promising.	Their son was named Olaf, and he was young and the most promising of all men.
Guðrún, kona Þórðar, var náskyld Bolla Bollasyni.	Gudrun, wife-of Thord, was closely-related Bolli Bollason.	Gudrun, Thord's wife, was closely related to Bolli Bollason.
Var hon systrungr hans.	Was she mother's-sister's-son his.	She was his cousin.
Óláfr, sonr þeira Þórðar, var heitinn eftir Óláfi pá í Hjarðarholti.	Olaf, son theirs Thord, was named after Olaf Peacock in Hjardarholt.	Their son Olaf was named after Olaf Peacock in Hjardarholt.
Þórðr ok Þorvaldr Hjaltasynir bjuggu at Hofi í Hjaltadal.	Thord and Thorvald Sons-of-Hjalti lived at Hof in Hjaltadal.	Thord and Thorvald Hjaltason lived at Hof in Hjaltadal.
Þeir váru höfðingjar miklir.	They were chieftains great.	They were great chieftains.
Maðr hét Þórólfr ok var kallaðr stertimaðr.	A-man was-named Thorolf and was called Stately-man.	There was a man named Thorolf and he was called Stuck-up.
Hann bjó í Þúfum.	He lived in Thufur.	He lived at Thufur.

The Tale of Bolli Bollason (Old Norse)

Old Norse	Literal	English
Hann var óvinveittr í skapi ok æðimaðr mikill.	He was unfriendly in mood and frenzy-man much.	He was unfriendly in nature and a very angry man.
Hann átti graðung grán, ólman.	He had a-bull grey, wild.	He had a wild grey bull.
Þórðr af Marbæli var í förum með Arnóri.	Thord of Marbaeli was on a-journey with Arnor.	Thord of Marbaeli was travelling with Arnor.
Þórólfr stærimaðr átti frændkonu Arnórs, en hann var þingmaðr Hjaltasona.	Thorolf Stately-man married kinswoman Arnor's, and he was assembly-man Hjaltasons.	Thorolf Stuck-up married one of Arnor's kinswomen, and was one of the assembly men of the Hjaltasons.
Hann átti illt við búa sína ok lagði þat í vanða sinn.	He had bad-terms with settlers his and became that in custom his.	He was on bad terms with his neighbours and that became the custom.
Kom þat mest til þeira Marbælinga.	Came that most to they-of Marbaeli.	And most of this came to the people of Marbaeli.
Graðungr hans gerði mönnum margt mein, þá er hann kom ór afréttum.	Bull his made people many harm, then as he came back-from the-pastures.	His bull did many people harm, when he came back from the pastures.
Meiddi hann fé manna, en gekk eigi undan grjóti.	Wounded he cattle people's, and went not away-from rocks.	He wounded people's cattle, and could not be made to go away with rocks.
Hann braut ok andvirki ok gerði margt illt.	He broke also haystacks and did much ill.	He also damaged haystacks and did much harm.
Þórðr af Marbæli hitti Þórólf at máli ok bað hann varðveita graðung sinn.	Thord of Marbaeli met Thorolf to discuss and asked him ward-knowing bull his.	Thord of Marbaeli met Thorolf to discuss this with him, and asked him to watch guard over his bull.
"Viljum vér eigi þola honum ofríki".	"Will we not endure his rampages".	"Will we not endure his rampages".
Þórólfr lézt eigi mundu sitja at fé sínu.	Thorolf said not would sit at cattle his.	Thorold said that he would not sit by his cattle.
Ferr Þórðr heim við svá búit.	Travelled Thord home with so prepared.	Thord travelled home with this reply.
Eigi miklu síðar getr Þórðr at líta, hvar graðungrinn hefir brotit niðr torfstakka hans.	Not much afterwards got Thord that look, where the-bull had broken down turf-stacks his.	Not long afterwards Thord noticed that the bull had torn apart his stacks of turf.

The Tale of Bolli Bollason (Old Norse)

Old Norse	Literal	English
Þórðr hleypr þá til ok hefir spjót í hendi, ok er boli sér þat, veðr hann jörð, svá at upp tekr um klaufir.	Thord ran then to and had spear in hand, and when the-bull saw that, weathered he earth, so that up took about hooves.	Thord then ran over with a spear in his hand, and when he saw it, the bull beat the ground and took up on his hooves.
Þórðr leggr til hans, svá at hann fellr dauðr á jörð.	Thord lunged to him, so that he fell dead to the-earth.	Thord lunged at him so that he fell dead on the ground.
Þórðr hittir Þórólf ok sagði honum, at boli var dauðr.	Thord met Thorolf and told him, that the-bull was dead.	Thord met Thorolf and told him, that the-bull was dead.
"Þetta var lítit frægðarverk", svarar Þórólfr, "en gera mynda ek þat vilja, er þér þætti eigi betr".	"This was little famous-work", answered Thorolf, "and do should I that will, that to-you seems not better".	"This deed is of little honour", answered Thorolf, "and I should wish to do to you something that is no better".
Þórólfr var málóði ok heitaðist í hverju orði.	Thorolf was of-violent-language and called at every word.	Thorolf called on violent language with every word.
Þórðr átti heimanferð fyrir höndum.	Thord had from-home-travel before his-hands.	Thord had to leave his farm.
Óláfr, sonr hans, var þá sjau vetra eða átta.	Olaf, son his, was then seven winters or eight.	His son Olaf was then seven or eight winters.
Hann fór af bænum með leik sínum ok gerði sér hús, sem börnum er títt, en Þórólfr kom þar at honum.	He went off the-farm with game his and made himself a-house, which children are reported, then Thorolf came there at him.	He went away from the farm and played a game of making himself a house, which children often do, and then Thorolf came at him.
Hann lagði sveininn í gegnum með spjóti.	He lunged the-boy in through with spear.	He lunged through the boy with a spear.
Síðan fór hann heim ok sagði konu sinni.	Afterwards travelled he home and told wife his.	Afterwards he travelled home and told his wife.
Hon svarar:	She answered:	She answered:
"Þetta er illt verk ok ómannligt.	"This is ill work and inhumane.	"This is an evil and inhumane deed.
Mun þér þetta illu reifa".	Shall you this evil account-for".	You shall account for this evil".

The Tale of Bolli Bollason (Old Norse)

Old Norse	Literal	English
En er hon tók á honum þungt, þá fór hann í brott þaðan ok létti eigi fyrr en hann kom á Miklabæ til Arnórs.	Since that she took of him negatively, then travelled he to away from-there and relieved not before that he came to Miklabaer to Arnor's.	Since she responded so negatively, he then travelled away and did not rest until he came to Miklabaer to Arnor.
Fréttust þeir tíðenda.	Reported they news.	They exchanged news.
Þórólfr segir honum víg Óláfs.	Thorolf told him slaying-of Olaf's.	Thorolf told him of the killing of Olaf.
"Sé ek þar nú til trausts, sem þér eruð, sakar mágsemðar".	"See I here now to trust, that you are, sake as-in-laws".	"I look here to trust in you, for my sake, as we are in-laws".
"Eigi ferr þú sjándi eftir um þenna hlut", sagði Arnórr, "at ek muna virða meira mágsemð við þik en virðing mína ok sæmð, ok ásjá áttu hér engrar ván af mér".	"Not going you seeing after about this lot", said Arnor, "that I should worth more in-laws with you than worth my and honour, and assistance have-you here none to-expect of me".	"You will not see it after this", said Arnor, "as I do not value my in-laws more than my honour, and you have no assistance to expect from me".
Fór Þórólfr upp eftir Hjaltadal til Hofs ok fann þá Hjaltasonu ok sagði þeim, hvar komit var hans máli, "ok sé ek hér nú til ásjá, sem þit eruð".	Travelled Thorolf up after Hjaltadal to Hof and found then Hjaltasons and told them, what came was his matter, "and being I here now to assistance, as you-two are".	Thorolf travelled for Hof in Hjaltadal and found the Hjaltasons and told them what had happened, "and I am here now to ask for your assistance, as you are".
Þórðr svarar:	Thord answered:	Thord answered:
"Slíkt eru níðingsverk, ok mun ek enga ásjá veita þér um þetta efni".	"Such is lowly-deed, and should I none assistance grant to-you about this matter".	"This is such a lowly deed, and I should grant you no assistance in this matter".
Þorvaldr varð um fár.	Thorvald was about few.	Thorvald was of few words.
Fær Þórólfr ekki af þeim at sinni.	Got Thorolf nothing from them in his.	Thorolf got nothing from them in this matter.
Reið hann í brott ok upp eftir Hjaltadal til Reykja, fór þar í laug.	Rode he to away and up after Hjaltadal to Reykir, went there to bathe.	He rode away for Hjaltadal to Reykir, where he went to bathe.

The Tale of Bolli Bollason (Old Norse)

Old Norse	Literal	English
En um kveldit reið hann ofan aftr ok undir virkit at Hofi ok ræddist við einn saman, svá sem annarr maðr væri fyrir ok kveddi hann ok frétti, hverr þar væri kominn.	Then about evening rode he down back and near the-compound at Hof and discussed with alone together, so as another man was before and greeting him and asking, who there was come.	Then in the evening he rode back down near the farmhouse at Hof where he spoke to himself, as if someone was standing there, who greeted him and asked who was there.
"Ek heiti Þórólfr", kvað hann.	"I am-named Thorolf", said he.	"I am named Thorolf", he said.
"Hvert vartu farinn, eða hvat er þér á höndum?" spyrr launmaðrinn.	"Which where travelling, and what is your in hand?" asked the-unseen-man.	"Where are you travelling, and what is your problem?" asked the unseen man.
Þórólfr segir tilfelli þessi öll, eftir því sem váru.	Thorolf told occurrence this all, after accordingly as was.	Thorolf told him all that had occurred.
"Bað ek Hjaltasonu ásjá", segir hann, "sakar nauðsynja minna".	"Asked I Hjaltasons assistance", said he, "for-the-sake-of deed-refuse mine".	"I asked for the Hjaltasons assistance", he said, "for the sake of my assistance".
Þessi svarar, er fyrir skyldi vera:	This answered, who before should be:	The man who should be before him answered:
"Gengit er nú þaðan, er þeir gerðu erfit þat it fjölmenna, er tólf hundruð manna sátu at, ok ganga slíkir höfðingjar mjök saman, er nú vilja eigi veita einum manni nökkura ásjá".	"Gone are now from-there, that they made difficulty that the many-men, were twelve hundred men sitting about, and went such chieftains many together, are now willing not grant any man any assistance".	"They are now gone, they who made the difficulty with many men, there were twelve hundred sitting about, and many such chieftains went together, who are not willing to grant any man assistance".
Þorvaldr var úti staddr ok heyrði talit.	Thorvald was outside standing and heard conversation.	Thorvald was standing outside and heard the conversation.
Hann gengr þangat til ok tók í tauma hestsins ok bað hann af baki stíga, "en þó er eigi virðingarvænligt við þik at eiga fyrir sakar fólsku þinnar".	He went there to and took the reins horse's and asked him off horseback step, "but though is not respect-kindly with you to have before conviction false yours".	He went over and took the reins of the horse and asked him to step off horseback, "but it is not with honour to help a man before me with a conviction as false as yours".

2

| *Nú er at segja frá Þórði, er hann kom heim ok frá víg sonar síns ok harmaði þat mjök.* | Now is to say from Thord, that he came home and from the-slaying-of son his and mourned that much. | Now the story turns to Thord, who came home and learned of the killing of his sun, and mourned it very much. |

The Tale of Bolli Bollason (Old Norse)

Old Norse	Literal	English
Guðrún, kona hans, mælti:	Gudrun, wife his, spoke:	His wife Gudrun spoke:
"Þat er þér ráð at lýsa vígi sveinsins á hönd Þórólfi, en ek mun ríða suðr til Tungu ok finna Bolla, frænda minn, ok vita, hvern styrk hann vill veita okkr til eftirmáls".	"It is to-you declare that describe the-slaying son-yours in hand Thorolf, and I should ride south to Tunga and find Bolli, kinsman mine, and know, what strength he wished grant us to after-matter".	"It is for you to declare Thorolf responsible for the slaying of your son, and I shall ride south to Tunga and find Bolli my kinsman, and know what help he is willing to grant us to gain redress".
Þau gerðu svá.	They did so.	This they did.
Ok er Guðrún kom í Tungu, fær hon þar viðtökur góðar.	And was Gudrun come to Tunga, travelled she there with-taking good.	And when Gudrun came to Tunga, she was given a good welcome.
Hon segir Bolla víg Óláfs, sonar síns, ok beiddi, at hann tæki við eftirmálinu.	She said Bolli killing Olaf's, son her, and asked, that he take with the-after-matter.	She told Bolli about the killing of her son Olaf, and asked that he take over the prosecution of the case.
Hann svarar:	He answered:	He answered:
"Eigi þykkir mér þetta svá hægligt, at seilast til sæmðar í hendr þeim Norðlendingum.	"Not seems to-me this so easily, to obtain to honour in hand they Northerners.	"It does not seem to me to be so easy, to obtain honour from those northerners.
Fréttist mér ok svá til sem maðrinn muni þar niðr kominn, at ekki muni hægt eftir at leita".	Reported me and so to that the-man should there down come, that not should possible after to seek".	It has been reported to me that this man has gone down somewhere that it will not be possible to seek him out.
Bolli tók þó við málinu um síðir, ok fór Guðrún norðr ok kom heim.	Bolli took though with the-case about eventually, and travelled Gudrun north and came home.	Bolli agreed to take on the case, and Gudrun travelled north and came home.
Hon sagði Þórði, bónda sínum, svá sem nú var komit, ok líðr svá fram um hríð.	She told Thord, husband hers, so as now was come, and passed so from about awhile.	When she arrived home, she told her husband Thord what had happened, and so it passed for a while.
Eftir jól um vetrinn var lagðr fundr í Skagafirði at Þverá, ok stefndi Þorvaldr þangat Guðdala-Starra.	After Yule about winter was laid a-meeting in Skagafjord at Thvera, and summoned Thorvald from-there Starri-of-Guddalir.	After Yule in winter there was a meeting held in Skagafjord at Thvera, and Thorvald summoned Starri of Guddalir.

The Tale of Bolli Bollason (Old Norse)

Old Norse	Literal	English
Hann var vinr þeira bræðra.	He was a-friend of-they the-brothers.	He was a friend of the (Hjaltason) brothers.
Þorvaldr fór til þingsins við sína menn, ok er þeir kómu fyrir Urðskriðuhóla, þá hljóp ór hlíðinni ofan at þeim maðr.	Thorvald travelled to the-assembly with his men, and when they came before Urdskriduholar, then ran from the-slope down at them a-man.	Thorvald travelled to the assembly with his men, and when they came to Urdskriduholar, a man came running down the slope towards them.
Var þar Þórólfr.	Was it Thorolf.	It was Thorolf.
Réðst hann í ferð með þeim Þorvaldi.	Rode he in travelling with them Thorvald.	He joined and rode with Thorvald (and his men).
Ok er þeir áttu skammt til Þverár, þá mælti Þorvaldr við Þórólf:	And when they had a-short-distance to Thvera, then spoke Thorvald with Thorolf:	When they had a short distance remaining to Thvera, Thorvald spoke to Thorolf:
"Nú skaltu hafa með þér þrjár merkr silfrs ok sitja hér upp frá bænum at Þverá.	"Now shall have with you three marks of-silver and sit here up from farmhouse at Thvera.	"Take three marks of silver and stay here above the farmhouse at Thvera.
Haf þat at marki, at ek mun snúa skildi mínum ok at þér holinu, ef þér er fritt, ok máttu þá fram ganga.	Have this as a-sign, that I shall turn shield mine and that you hollow, if you are safe, and may then from go.	Have this as a sign, that I will turn the inside of my shield if you are safe and can come from there.
Skjöldrinn er hvítr innan".	The-shield is white inside".	The shield is white on the inside".
Ok er Þorvaldr kom til þingsins, hittust þeir Starri ok tóku tal saman.	And when Thorvald came to the-assembly, met they Starri and took-to talking together.	And when Thorvald came to the assembly, they met Starri and talked together.
Þorvaldr mælti:	Thorvald spoke:	Thorvald spoke:
"Svá er mál með vexti, at ek vil þess beiða, at þú takir við Þórólfi stærimanni til varðveizlu ok trausts.	"So is the-matter with grown, that I will this offer, that you take with Thorolf Stately-man to hospitality and trust.	"So is the matter has come, I will offer this, that I wish you to take Thorolf Stuck-up into your hospitality and support.
Mun ek fá þér þrjár merkr silfrs ok vináttu mína".	Should I fee to-you three marks of-silver and friendship mine".	I shall pay you three marks of silver and give you my friendship.

The Tale of Bolli Bollason (Old Norse)

Old Norse	Literal	English
"Þar er sá maðr", svarar Starri, "er mér þykkir ekki vinsæll, ok óvíst, at honum fylgi hamingja.	"There is so a-man", answered Starri, "that to-me seems not popular, and uncertain, that he follows luck.	"There is such a man", answered Starri, "that is not popular in my eyes, and not likely to bring much luck.
En sakar okkars vinskapar þá vil ek við honum taka".	But for-the-sake-of our friendship then will I with him take".	But for the sake of our friendship I will take him with me".
"Þá gerir þú vel", segir Þorvaldr.	"The do you well", said Thorvald.	"You do well in that case", said Thorvald.
Sneri hann þá skildinum ok frá sér hválfinu, ok er Þórólfr sér þat, gengr hann fram, ok tók Starri við honum.	Turned he then the-shield and from himself half, and when Thorolf saw that, went he from, and took Starri with him.	He then turned his shield from himself half way, and when Thorolf saw that, he went from where he was and received him.
Starri átti jarðhús í Guðdölum, því at jafnan váru með honum skógarmenn.	Starri had earth-house in Guddalir, because that usually were with him forest-men.	Starri had an earth house in Guddalir because he usually had outlaws with him.
Átti hann ok nökkut sökótt.	Had he also some accusations.	He had also had some charges against him.

3 | # 3 | # 3

Bolli Bollason býr til vígsmálit Óláfs.	Bolli Son-of-Bolli prepared to fight-the-case Olaf's.	Bolli Bollason prepared to prosecute Olaf's case.
Hann býst heiman ok ferr norðr til Skagafjarðar með þrjá tigu manna.	He prepared at-home and set-out north to Skagafjord with three ten men.	He made preparations and set out north to Skagafjord with thirty men.
Hann kemr á Miklabæ, ok er honum þar vel fagnat.	He came to Miklabaer, and was he there well welcomed.	He came to Miklabaer and was well welcomed there.
Segir hann, hversu af stóð um ferðir hans.	Said he, how-so of stood about journey his.	He told them the reasons for his journey.
"Ætla ek at hafa fram vígsmálit nú á Hegranessþingi á hendr Þórólfi stærimanni.	"Intend I to have from fight-the-case now to Hegranes-Assembly in hand Thorolf Stately-man.	"I intend to prosecute the case at Hegranes Assembly for Thorolf Stuck-up.
Vilda ek, at þú værir mér um þetta mál liðsinnaðr".	Wish I, that you would-be to-me about this matter team-minded".	I would like you to assist and cooperate with me in this matter".

The Tale of Bolli Bollason (Old Norse)

Old Norse	Literal	English
Arnórr svarar:	Arnor answered:	Arnor answered:
"Ekki þykkir mér þú, Bolli, vænt stefna út, er þú sækir norðr hingat, við slíka ójafnaðarmenn sem hér er at eiga.	"Not seems to-me you, Bolli, expect agreement from, that you seek north here, with such un-equal-men which here are to in.	"It doesn't seems to me, Bolli, that you can expect an agreement that you seek here in the north, with such unjust men that are here".
Munu þeir þetta mál meir verja með kappi en réttendum.	Should they this matter more protect with warriors whether right.	They would defend this matter as warriors whether just or unjust.
En ærin nauðsyn þykkir mér þér á vera.	But considerable necessity seems to-me to-you to be.	But it seems that you have a considerable necessity.
Munum vér ok freista, at þetta mál gangi fram".	Should we also try, that this matter going from".	So we should try to do what we can in this matter.
Arnórr dregr at sér fjölmenni mikit.	Arnor drew to himself followers-many much.	Arnor collected a large number of men.
Ríða þeir Bolli til þingsins.	Rode they Bolli to the-assembly.	They rode with Bolli to the assembly.
Þeir bræðr fjölmenna mjök til Hegranesþings.	The brothers following-men much to Hegranes-Assembly.	The brothers also came with many followers to Hegranes Assembly.
Þeir hafa frétt um ferðir Bolla.	They had news about journey Bolli's.	They had news about Bolli's journey.
Ætla þeir at verja málit.	Intended they to defend the-case.	They intended to defend the case.
Ok er menn koma til þingsins, hefir Bolli fram sakar á hendr Þórólfi,	And when people came to the-assembly, had Bolli from the-charges in hand Thorolf,	And when people came to the assembly, Bolli presented the charges against Thorolf,
ok er til varna var boðit, gengu þeir til Þorvaldr ok Starri við sveit sína ok hugðu at eyða málinu fyrir Bolla með styrk ok ofríki.	and was to defence was bid, went they to Thorvald and Starri with company theirs and thought that devastate the-case before Bolli with strength and un-rule.	and then the defence was made, and Thorvald and Starri came forward with their company, they intended to block Bolli's prosecution with strength and unruliness.
En er þetta sér Arnórr, gengr hann í milli með sína sveit ok mælti:	Then when this saw Arnor, went he in between with his company and spoke:	Then when Arnor saw this, he went in-between with his company and spoke:

The Tale of Bolli Bollason (Old Norse)

Old Norse	Literal	English
"Þat er mönnum einsætt at færa hér eigi svá marga góða menn í vandræði sem á horfist, at menn skyli eigi ná lögum um mál sín.	"It is to-people one-agreement that bringing here not so many good men in dispute as to looks, that people shall not obtain law about the-matter this.	"It is clear that so many good men should not be here in the dispute as now looks likely, that people shall not get justice in this matter.
Er ok ófallit at fylgja Þórólfi um þetta mál.	It-is also misguided to follow Thorolf about this case.	It is also misguided to support Thorolf in this case.
Muntu, Þorvaldr, ok óliðdrjúgr verða, ef reyna skal".	Should-you, Thorvald, also un-substantial-company become, if tested shall-be".	And you, Thorvald, will have little backing if it comes to a show of force.
Þeir Þorvaldr ok Starri sá nú, at málit myndi fram ganga, því at þeir höfðu ekki liðsafla við þeim Arnóri ok léttu þeir frá.	They Thorvald and Starri saw now, that the-case should from go, since that they had not company-provided with them Arnor and relieved they from.	Thorvald and Starri now saw that the case would be concluded, since they did not have the same number of men with them to match Arnor, so they withdrew.
Bolli sekði Þórólf stærimann þar á Hegranessþingi um víg Ólafs, frænda síns, ok fór við þat heim.	Bolli convicted Thorolf Stately-man there at Hegranes-Assembly about the-killing-of Olaf's, kinsman his, and travelled with that home.	Bolli convicted Thorolf Stuck-up there at Hegranes Assembly for the killing of his kinsman Olaf, and then went home.
Skilðust þeir Arnórr með kærleik.	Separated they Arnor with friendship.	He separated from Arnor with friendship.
Sat Bolli í búi sínu.	Sat Bolli in farm his.	Bolli stayed on his farm.

4   4   4

Old Norse	Literal	English
Þorgrímr hét maðr.	Thorgrim was-named a-man.	There was a man named Thorgrim.
Hann átti skip uppi standanda í Hrútafirði.	He had a-ship up stood in Hrutafjord.	He had a ship which stood at Hrutafjord.
Þangat reið Starri ok Þórólfr við honum.	There rode Starri and Thorolf to him.	Starri and Thorolf rode there to be with him.
Starri mælti við stýrimann:	Starri spoke with the-captain:	Starri spoke with the captain:

The Tale of Bolli Bollason (Old Norse)

Old Norse	Literal	English
"Hér er maðr, at ek vil, at þú takir við ok flytir útan, ok hér eru þrjár merkr silfrs, er þú skalt hafa ok þar með vináttu mína".	"Here is a-man, that I wish, that you take with and with-fleetness abroad, and here are three marks of-silver, and you shall have also there with friendship mine".	"Here is a man that I wish you to take abroad quickly, and here are three marks of silver, and you shall also have my friendship".
Þorgrímr mælti:	Thorgrim spoke:	Thorgrim spoke:
"Á þessu þykkir mér nökkurr vandi, hversu af hendi verðr leyst.	"About this seems to-me somewhat difficulty, how-so of hand becomes solved.	"It seems to me that it will be somewhat difficult to be able to solve.
En við áskorun þína mun ek við honum taka,	But with challenge yours should I with him take,	But with your challenge I shall take him,
en þó þykkir mér þessi maðr vera ekki giftuvænligr".	but though seems to-me this a-man becomes not luck-promised".	though it seems to me that this man promises much luck".
Þórólfr réðst nú í sveit með kaupmönnum, en Starri ríðr heim við svá búit.	Thorolf rode now in company with trading-men, and Starri rode home with so prepared.	Thorolf then rode in company with the merchants, and Starri rode home so prepared.
Nú er at segja frá Bolla.	Now is to say from Bolli.	Now the story turns to Bolli.
Hann hugsar nú efni þeira Þórólfs ok þykkir eigi verða mjök með öllu fylgt, ef Þórólfr skal sleppa.	He thought now the-matter theirs Thorolf's and thought not would-be much with all followed, if Thorolf should escape.	He thought about their matter with Thorolf and thought it would not be much if it followed that Thorolf should escape.
Frétti hann nú, at hann er til skips riðinn.	Learned he now, that he was to ships riding.	He now learned that he was riding to the ships.
Bolli býst heiman.	Bolli prepared from-home.	Bolli prepared to leave home.
Setr hann hjálm á höfuð sér, skjöld á hlið,	Set he helmet on head his, shield about side,	He put his helmet on his head, his shield by his side,
spjót hafði hann í hendi, en gyrðr sverðinu Fótbít.	spear had he in hand, in buckled the-sword Leg-Biter.	his spear in his hand, and buckled the sword Leg Biter.
Hann ríðr norðr til Hrútafjarðar ok kom í þat mund, er kaupmenn váru albúnir.	He rode north to Hrutafjord and came in so about-that-time, as trading-men were all-prepared.	He rode north to Hrutafjord and arrived at about the time that the merchants were all prepared.

The Tale of Bolli Bollason (Old Norse)

Old Norse	Literal	English
Var þá ok vindr á kominn.	Then when also the-wind up came.	Then the wind also came up.
Ok er Bolli reið at búðardurunum, gekk Þórólfr út í því ok hafði húðfat í fangi sér.	And as Bolli rode to the-booth-doors, went Thorolf out about because also had bed-roll in arms his.	And as Bolli rode up to the camp doors, Thorolf came out carrying his bed roll in his arms.
Bolli bregðr Fótbít ok leggr í gegnum hann.	Bolli drew Leg-Biter and lunged at through him.	Bolli drew Leg Biter and lunged through him.
Fellr Þórólfr á bak aftr í búðina inn, en Bolli hleypr á hest sinn.	Fell Thorolf on back down in the-booth inside, and Bolli ran to horse his.	Thorolf fell back into the camp, and Bolli ran to his horse.
Kaupmenn hljópu saman ok at honum.	Trading-men ran together and at him.	The merchants ran together towards him.
Bolli mælti:	Bolli spoke:	Bolli spoke:
"Hitt er yðr ráðligast at láta nú vera kyrrt, því at yðr mun ofstýri verða at leggja mik við velli,	"Find is you advisable that leave now being peace, because that you should unmanageable being to lay me with the-fields,	"It is advisable that you leave now in peace, because you shall not manage to bring me down in the fields,
en vera má, at ek kvista einhvern yðvarn eða alla tvá, áðr ek em felldr".	but being may, that I trim one of-you or all two, before I am falling".	and it may be, that I trim one or two of you before I fall".
Þorgrímr segir:	Thorgrim said:	Thorgrim said:
"Ek hygg, at þetta sé satt".	"I think, that this is true".	"I think that this is true".
Létu þeir vera kyrrt, en Bolli reið heim ok hefir sótt mikinn frama í þessi ferð.	Let they be still, and Bolli rode home and had attended much honour in this journey.	They remained still, and Bolli rode home and earned a great deal of honour from this journey.
Fær hann af þessu virðing mikla, ok þótti mönnum farit sköruliga, hefir sekðan manninn í öðrum fjórðungi, en síðan riðit einn saman í hendr óvinum sínum ok drepit hann þar.	Accomplished he of this honour much, and thought people travelled boldly, had outlawed person in another district, and then ride alone together in hand un-friends his and kill him there.	He accomplished much honour in this, and people thought he travelled boldly, to have the man outlawed in another district, and then riding alone into the hands of his enemies and killing him there.

The Tale of Bolli Bollason (Old Norse)

Old Norse	Literal	English
# 5	# 5	# 5
Um sumarit á alþingi fundust þeir Bolli ok Guðmundr inn ríki ok töluðu margt.	About summer at the-assembly met they Bolli and Gudmund the powerful and talked much.	About summer at the assembly Bolli and Gudmund the Powerful met and talked much.
Þá mælti Guðmundr;	Then spoke Gudmund;	Then Gudmund spoke:
"Því vil ek lýsa, Bolli, at ek vil við slíka menn vingast sem þér eruð.	"Because wish I show, Bolli, that I wish with such people make-friends as you are.	"I wish to say to you, Bolli, that I wish to make friends with people like you.
Ek vil bjóða þér norðr til mín til hálfsmánaðar veizlu, ok þykkir mér betr, at þú komir".	I wish to-invite you north to mine to half-month's feast, and consider me better, that you come".	I wish to invite you north to mine for a half month's feast, and I would think the best of it if you came".
Bolli svarar, at vísu vill hann þiggja sæmðir at slíkum manni, ok hét hann ferðinni.	Bolli answered, that certainly wished he accept honour from such a-man, and promised he the-journey.	Bolli answered that he certainly wished to accept this honour from such a man, and promised that he would make the journey.
Þá urðu ok fleiri menn til at veita honum þessi vinganarmál.	Then became also more men to that grant him this friendship-matter.	Then others also came to grant him friendship.
Arnórr kerlingarnef bauð Bolla ok til veizlu á Miklabæ.	Arnor Crone's-nose invited Bolli also to feast at Miklabaer.	Arnor Crone's-Nose also invited Bolli to a feast at Miklabaer.
Maðr hét Þorsteinn.	A-man named Thorstein.	There was a man named Thorstein.
Hann bjó at Hálsi.	He lived at Hals.	He lived at Hals.
Hann var sonr Hellu-Narfa.	He was the-son-of Hellu-Narfi.	He was the son of Hellu-Narfi.
Hann bauð Bolla til sín, er hann færi norðan, ok Þórðr á Marbæli bauð Bolla.	He invited Bolli to his, that he travel north, and Thord at Marbaeli invited Bolli.	He invited Bolli to travel north to his, and so did Thord at Marbaeli.
Fóru menn af þinginu, ok reið Bolli heim.	Travelled people to the-assembly, and rode Bolli home.	People travelled to the assembly, and Bolli rode home.
Þetta sumar kom skip í Dögurðarnes ok settist þar upp.	That summer came a-ship in Dagverdarnes and set there up.	That summer a ship came in at Dagverdarnes and set up there.
Bolli tók til vistar í Tungu tólf kaupmenn.	Bolli took to lodging at Tunga twelve trading-men.	Bolli took lodging for twelve trading men.

The Tale of Bolli Bollason (Old Norse)

Old Norse	Literal	English
Váru þeir þar um vetrinn, ok veitti Bolli þeim allstórmannliga.	Were they there about winter, and granted Bolli home all-great-man-like.	They were there about winter, and Bolli provided from them generously.
Sátu þeir um kyrrt fram yfir jól.	Sat they about still from over Yule.	They stayed there for Yule.
En eftir jól ætlar Bolli at vitja heimboðanna norðr, ok lætr hann þá járna hesta ok býr ferð sína.	Then after Yule intended Bolli to visit home-invitation north, and had he then iron-shod horses and prepared travel his.	Then after Yule, Bolli intended to visit the north as invited, and he had horses shod and prepared to travel.
Váru þeir átján í reið.	Were they eighteen in riding.	There were eighteen of them riding.
Váru kaupmenn allir vápnaðir.	Were trading-men all weaponed.	All the merchants were armed.
Bolli reið í blári kápu ok hafði í hendi spjótit konungsnaut, it góða.	Bolli rode in black cape and had in hand spear king's-gift, the good.	Bolli rode in a black cape and in his hand the spear, King's Gift, the good.
Þeir ríða nú norðr ok koma á Marbæli til Þórðar.	They rode now north and came to Marbaeli to Thord.	They now rode north and came to Marbaeli to Thord.
Var þar allvel við þeim tekit, sátu þrjár nætr í miklum fagnaði.	Were there all-well with them taken, sat three nights in much celebration.	They were all well received and stayed three nights in celebration.
Þaðan riðu þeir á Miklabæ til Arnórs, ok tók hann ágætliga vel við þeim.	From-there rode they to Miklabaer to Arnor's, and took him greatly well with them.	From there they rode to Miklabaer to Arnor, and he received them well.
Var þar veizla in bezta.	Was there the-feast the best.	There was the best feast.
Þá mælti Arnórr:	Then spoke Arnor:	Then Arnor spoke:
"Vel hefir þú gert, Bolli, er þú hefir mik heimsótt.	"Well have you done, Bolli, that you have my home-sought.	"You have done well, Bolli, for seeking my home.
Þykkir mér þú hafa lýst í því við mik mikinn félagsskap.	Think I you have shown it therefore with me much comradeship.	I think you have therefore shown me much comradeship.
Skulu eigi eftir betri gjafar með mér en þú skalt þiggja mega.	Shall not after better gifts with me than you shall accept may.	And no better gifts will remain here with me that the ones you accept at parting.

The Tale of Bolli Bollason (Old Norse)

Old Norse	Literal	English
Mín vinátta skal þér ok heimul vera.	My friendship shall to-you also have-right be.	My friendship is also yours for the asking.
En nökkurr grunr er mér á, at þér sé eigi allir menn hliðhollir í þessu heraði, þykkjast sviptir vera sæmðum.	But somewhat suspect that for-me about, that you being not all men open-whole in this district, think loss being honour.	But I suspect that around me, not everyone in this district is inclined towards you, thinking that they have lost their honour.
Kemr þat mest til þeira Hjaltasona.	Coming that most to they Hjaltasons.	Most of that coming to the Hjaltasons.
Mun ek nú ráðast til ferðar með þér norðr á Heljardalsheiði, þá er þér farið heðan".	Should I now arrange to travel with you north to Heljardal Heath, then when you travel from-here".	I shall now arrange to travel north with you to Herjardal Heath when you leave here".
Bolli svarar:	Bolli answered:	Bolli answered:
"Þakka vil ek yðr, Arnórr bóndi, alla sæmð, er þér gerið til mín nú ok fyrrum.	"Thanks wish I you, Arnor host, all honour, that you do about mine now and before-us.	"I wish to thank you, Arnor my host, for all the honour, that you have shown me now before us.
Þykkir mér ok þat bæta várn flokk, at þér ríðið með oss.	Seems to-me also that better our flock, that you ride with us.	It seems to me better for our flock, if you ride with us.
En allt hugðum vér at fara með spekð um þessi heruð,	Then all think we that travel with wisdom about this district,	Then we think we will travel with wisdom through this district,
en ef aðrir leita á oss, þá má vera, at vér leikim þá enn nökkut í mót".	that if others look for us, then may be, that we sport then but somewhat in meeting".	so that if others look for us, as they may, then we will give them some sport in meeting us".
Síðan ræðst Arnórr til ferðar með þeim, ok ríða nú veg sinn.	Afterwards rode Arnor to travel with them, and rode now way theirs.	Afterwards Arnor prepared to ride with them, and they set out on their way.

6

Nú er at segja frá Þorvaldi, at hann tekr til orða við Þórð, bróður sinn:	Now is to say from Thorvald, that he took to words with Thord, brother his:	Now the story turns to Thorvald, that he spoke to his brother Thord:
"Vita muntu, at Bolli ferr heðra at heimboðum.	"Know shall-you, that Bolli travels district at home-invitations.	"You know that Bolli travels in this district going to home invitations.

The Tale of Bolli Bollason (Old Norse)

Old Norse	Literal	English
Eru þeir nú at Arnórs átján saman ok ætla norðr Heljardalsheiði".	Are they now at Arnor's eighteen together and intend north Heljardal Heath".	There are eighteen of then together, and they intend north to Herjardal Heath.
"Veit ek þat", svarar Þórðr.	"Know I that", answered Thord.	"I know that", answered Thord.
Þorvaldr mælti:	Thorvald spoke:	Thorvald said:
"Ekki er mér þó um þat, at Bolli hlaupi hér svá um horn oss, at vér finnim hann eigi, því at ek veit eigi, hverr minni sæmð hefir meir niðr drepit en hann".	"Not am I though about that, that Bolli running here so about horn ours, that we find him not, such that I know none, who diminish honour has more down killing than him".	"I am not happy with the idea that Bolli is running around here under our noses, and we don't go to meet him, because I know no one, who has diminished my honour more than him".
Þórðr mælti:	Thord spoke:	Thord spoke:
"Mjök ertu íhlutunarsamr ok meir en ek vilda, ok ófarin myndi þessi, ef ek réða.	"Great are-you in-sharing-together also more than I wish, and un-faring should this, if I decide.	"You are great at sharing in things more than I wish, and this should not go, if I am the one to decide.
Þykkir mér óvíst, at Bolli sé ráðlauss fyrir þér".	Seems to-me uncertain, that Bolli so ill-advised for you".	It seems uncertain to me, that Bolli would be so ill-advised about you".
"Eigi mun ek letjast láta", svarar Þorvaldr, "en þú munt ráða ferð þinni".	"Not should I dissuaded allow", answered Thorvald, "but you should decide travel yours".	"I should not allow that to dissuade me", answered Thorvald, "but you should decide your course".
Þórðr mælti:	Thord spoke:	Third spoke:
"Eigi mun ek eftir sitja, ef þú ferr, bróðir, en þér munum vér eigna alla virðing, þá er vér hljótum í þessi ferð, ok svá, ef öðruvís berr til".	"Not should I after sitting, if you travel, brother, but you shall we own all worthiness, then as we we-get in this journey, and so, if other-knowing bear to".	"I shall not stay, if you travel, brother, but you shall own all the honour we may get from this journey, or any other consequences".
Þorvaldr safnar at sér mönnum, ok verða þeir átján saman ok ríða á leið fyrir þá Bolla ok ætla at sitja fyrir þeim.	Thorvald collected for his men, and became they eighteen together and rode to journey for then Bolli and intended to sit before them.	Thorvald collected together his men to become a party of eighteen and together they rode on the journey that Bolli made and intended to sit in ambush before them.
Þeir Arnórr ok Bolli ríða nú með sína menn.	They Arnor and Bolli rode now with their men.	Arnor and Bolli rode with their men.

The Tale of Bolli Bollason (Old Norse)

Old Norse	Literal	English
Ok er skammt var í milli þeira ok Hjaltasona, þá mælti Bolli til Arnórs:	And when short-distance were in between them and Hjaltasons, then spoke Bolli to Arnor's:	And when there was a short distance between them and the Hjaltasons, Bolli said to Arnor:
"Mun eigi þat nú ráð, at þér hverfið aftr? Hafið þér þó fylgt oss it drengiligsta.	"Should not is now advised, that you turn back?" Have you though followed us the bravely.	"Should it not now be advised that you turn back? Though you have followed us bravely.
Munu þeir Hjaltasynir ekki sæta fláráðum við mik".	Should they Hjaltasons not sit-in-ambush treacherous with me".	The Hjaltasons should not sit in ambush for me in treachery".
Arnórr mælti:	Arnor spoke:	Arnor spoke:
"Eigi mun ek enn aftr hverfa, því at svá er sem annarr segi mér, at Þorvaldr muni til þess ætla at hafa fund þinn,	"Not should I then back turn, because that so is that another say me, that Thorvald should to this intend to have meet you,	"I shall not turn back, because something tells me that Thorvald intends to meet you,
eða hvat sé ek þar upp koma? Blika þar eigi skildir við? Ok munu þar vera Hjaltasynir.	and what see I there up coming? Shining there not shields with?" And should there be Hjaltasons.	and what is that I see moving there? Is that not the glimmer of shields? That will be the Hjaltasons.
En þó mætti nú svá um búast, at þessi þeira ferð yrði þeim til engrar virðingar, en megi metast fjörráð við þik".	But though may now so about prepare, that this they travel with them to no honour, but may meet plotting against you".	But now shall we be prepared, that they will travel with no honour, that they are plotting against you".
Nú sjá þeir Þorvaldr bræðr, at þeir Bolli eru hvergi liðfæri en þeir, ok þykkjast sjá, ef þeir sýna nökkura óhæfu af sér, at þeira kostr myndi mikit versna.	Now saw they Thorvald brothers, that they Bolli were neither company-less than they, and realised saw, if they seemed somewhat unqualified of themselves, that they chose would much worse.	Thorvald and his brother saw that Bolli and his company were no less in numbers than they were, and when they saw this they realised, that if they were unqualified themselves, that the choice of aggression would be much worse.
Sýnist þeim þat ráðligast at snúa aftr, alls þeir máttu ekki sínum vilja fram koma.	Seemed to-them that advice that return back, all they may not theirs will from coming.	It seemed to them that the best advice was now to turn back, since they were not able to carry out their will.
Þá mælti Þórðr:	Then spoke Thord:	Then Thord spoke:

The Tale of Bolli Bollason (Old Norse)

Old Norse	Literal	English
"Nú fór sem mik varði, at þessi ferð myndi verða hæðilig, ok þætti mér enn betra heima setit,	"Now goes as much expect, that this journey would become mockery, and seems to-me the better home stay,	"Now it goes as I expected, that this journey would make a mockery of us, and it seems better if we had stayed at home,
höfum sýnt oss í fjandskap við menn, en komit engu á leið".	has shown us in fiendship with people, but come nothing from passed".	we have shown hostility with people, but achieved nothing".
Þeir Bolli ríða leið sína.	They Bolli rode way theirs.	Bolli and his men rode their way.
Fylgir Arnórr þeim upp á heiðina, ok skilði hann eigi fyrr við þá en hallaði af norðr.	Followed Arnor them up to the-heath, and separated he not before with then but turned of north.	Arnor followed them up to the heath, and did not leave them until they turned north.
Þá hvarf hann aftr, en þeir riðu ofan eftir Svarfaðardal ok kómu á bæ þann, er á Skeiði heitir.	Then broke-away he back, but they rode down along Svarfadardal and came to a-farm then, which was Skeid named.	Then he broke away and returned home while they rode down through Svarfadardal until they reached a farm called Skeid.
Þar bjó sá maðr, er Helgi hét.	There lived so a-man, who Helgi named.	There lived a man there who was named Helgi.
Hann var ættsmár ok illa í skapi, auðigr at fé.	He was of-family-small and bad in mood, rich in wealth.	He was not from a good family, ill-tempered, but wealthy.
Hann átti þá konu, er Sigríðr hét.	He had then wife, who Sigrid named.	He had a wife named Sigrid.
Hon var frændkona Þorsteins Hellu-Narfasonar.	She was kinswoman Thorstein's Hellu-Narfason.	The was a kinswoman of Thorstein Hellu-Narfason.
Hon var þeira skörungr meiri.	She was of-them noble the-more.	She was the more outstanding of them.
Þeir Bolli litu heygarð hjá sér.	There Bolli looked hay-stacks beside them.	Bolli looked and saw hay stacks nearby.
Stigu þeir þar af baki, ok kasta þeir fyrir hesta sína ok verja til heldr litlu, en þó helt Bolli þeim aftr at heygjöfinni.	Dismounted they there off horseback, and cast there before horses theirs and guarding to rather little, but though held Bolli they back the hay-giving.	They dismounted their horses, and cast them before the horses, taking rather little, and Bolli restrained them even more.

The Tale of Bolli Bollason (Old Norse)

Old Norse	Literal	English
"Veit ek eigi", segir hann, "hvert skaplyndi bóndi hefir".	"Know I not", said he, "what nature the-farmer has".	"I don't know", he said, "what sort of nature this farmer has".
Þeir gáfu heyvöndul ok létu hestana grípa í.	They gave hay-bundle and led the-horses grab to.	They took handfuls of hay and let the horses eat them.
Á bænum heima gekk út maðr ok þegar inn aftr ok mælti:	About the-farm home went out a-man and from-there inside returned and spoke:	About the farm came out a man from inside who went back inside and spoke:
"Menn eru við heygarð þinn, bóndi, ok reyna desjarnar".	"Men are with hay-stacks yours, farmer, and trying the-hay".	"Men are at your haystacks, master, trying the hay".
Sigríðr húsfreyja svarar:	Sigrid housewife answered:	Sigrid the housewife answered,
"Þeir einir munu þar menn vera, at þat mun ráð at spara eigi hey við".	"They only would there men be, that it would decide to spare not hey with".	"The only men who will be there, are those that it will be a good idea not to spare hay".
Helgi hljóp upp í óðafári ok kvað aldri hana skyldu þessu ráða, at hann léti stela heyjum sínum.	Helgi leapt up in a-hurry and said never he should this allow, that he let steal hay his.	Helgi leapt up in a hurry and said that he would never allow others to steal his hay.
Hann hleypr þegar, sem hann sé vitlauss, ok kemr þar at, sem þeir áðu.	He ran immediately, as-if he was wit-less, and came there to, as they to.	He ran out immediately as if he were crazed, and came up to where the men were.
Bolli stóð upp, er hann leit ferðina mannsins, ok studdist við spjótit konungsnaut.	Bolli stood up, as he saw going the-man, and stood with the-spear king's-gift.	Bolli stood up as he saw the man coming, and stood up with the help of the spear, King's Gift.
Ok þegar Helgi kom at honum, mælti hann:	And as-soon-as Helgi came to him, spoke he:	As soon as Helgi reached him, he spoke:
"Hverir eru þessir þjófarnir, er mér bjóða ofríki ok stela mik eign minni ok rífa í sundr hey mitt fyrir fararskjóta sína?"	"Who are these thieves, that me offer unruly and stealing my own less and tearing to asunder hay mine for horses theirs?"	"Who are these thieves, that harass me and steal what is mine and tearing apart my hay for their horses?".
Bolli segir nafn sitt.	Bolli said name his.	Bolli told him his name.
Helgi svarar:	Helgi answered:	Helgi answered:
"Þat er óliðligt nafn, ok muntu vera óréttvíss".	"That is unsuitable name, and should-you be un-right-knowing".	"That is an unsuitable name, and you must be an unjust man".

The Tale of Bolli Bollason (Old Norse)

Old Norse	Literal	English
"Vera má, at svá sé", segir Bolli, "en hinu skaltu mæta, er réttvísi er í".	"Be-it may, that so this", said Bolli, "but the shall-you meet, which right-knowing that is".	"It may be that it is", said Bolli, "but you shall have your justice".
Bolli keyrði þá hestana frá heyinu ok bað þá eigi æja lengr.	Bolli spurred then horses from the-hay and ordered then none rest any-longer.	Bolli then spurred the horses away from the hay, and ordered that none would rest there any longer.
Helgi mælti:	Helgi spoke:	Helgi spoke:
"Ek kalla yðr hafa stolit mik þessu, sem þér hafið haft, ok gert á hendr yðr skóggangssök".	"I declare you have stolen mine this, as you have had, and done in hand your forest-seeking".	"I declare you have stolen what is mine, which you have, and you have committed an offence to outlawry".
"Þú munt vilja, bóndi", sagði Bolli, "at vér komim fyrir oss fébótum við þik, ok hafir þú eigi sakar á oss.	"You should wish, farmer", said Bolli, "that we come before us compensation with you, and have you no conviction of us.	"You will want, farmer", said Bolli, "that we bring forth compensation with you, so that you will have no conviction with us.
Mun ek gjalda tvenn verð fyrir hey þitt".	Shall I pay twice the-worth for hay yours".	I shall pay twice the worth of your hay".
"Þat ferr heldr fjarri", svarar hann, "mun ek framar á hyggja um þat, er vér skiljum".	"That goes behind far-away", answered he, "should I honour to think about that, which our understanding".	"That is nowhere near enough", he answered, "I should think about my honour, what understanding we shall have".
Bolli mælti:	Bolli spoke:	Bolli spoke:
"Eru nökkurir hlutir þeir, bóndi, er þú vilir hafa í sætt af oss?"	"Are-there some things they, farmer, that you wish to-have to settle of us?"	"Are there any objects, farmer, that you wish to have to settle with us?".
"Þat þykkir mér vera mega", svarar Helgi, "at ek vilja spjót þat it gullrekna, er þú hefir í hendi".	"That think I be may", answered Helgi, "that I wish spear that the gold-inlaid, that you have in hand".	"I think it might be", answered Helgi, "that I wish to have the spear that is inlaid with gold, that you have in your hand".
"Eigi veit ek", sagði Bolli, "hvárt ek nenni þat til at láta.	"Not know I", said Bolli, "whether I care that to have allow.	"I do not know", said Bolli, "whether I care to allow that.
Hefi ek annat nökkut heldr fyrir því ætlat.	Have I another something rather for therefore intended.	I have some other intentions with it.

The Tale of Bolli Bollason (Old Norse)

Old Norse	Literal	English
Máttu þat ok varla tala at beiðast vápns ór hendi mér.	May that also barely speak to ask weapons from-out-of hand mine.	You could hardly speak to ask for a weapon from my hand.
Tak heldr annat fé svá mikit, at þú þykkist vel haldinn af".	Take rather another fee so much, that you think well holds of".	Take instead as much money as you consider that you are well off".
"Fjarri ferr þat", svarar Helgi, "er þat ok bezt, at þér svarið slíku fyrir sem þér hafið til gert".	"Far-away goes that", answered Helgi, "is it also best, that you answer such for as you have to done".	"Far be it from me", answered Helgi, "it is best that you answer for what you have done".
Síðan hóf Helgi upp stefnu ok stefndi Bolla um þjófnað ok lét varða skóggang.	Then began Helgi upped summons and charged Bolli with theft and had warranted outlawry.	Then Helgi started a lawsuit and sued Bolli for theft and had a warranted outlawry.
Bolli stóð ok heyrði til ok brosti við lítinn þann.	Bolli stood and heard to and laughed against a-little then.	Bolli stood and listened and laughed a little.
En er Helgi hafði lokit stefnunni, mælti hann:	Then when Helgi had finished the-summons, spoke he:	But when Helgi had finished the summons, he said:
"Nær fórtu heiman?"	"When travelled-you from-home?"	"When did you leave home?".
Bolli sagði honum.	Bolli told him.	Bolli told him.
Þá mælti bóndi:	Then spoke the-farmer:	Then the farmer said:
"Þá tel ek þik hafa á öðrum alizt meir en hálfan mánuð".	"Then say I you have of others homes more than half a-month".	"Then I think you have been living off others for more than half a month".
Helgi hefr þá upp aðra stefnu ok stefnir Bolla um verðgang.	Helgi had then upped another summons and charged Bolli with vagrancy.	Helgi had then brought up another summons and charged Bolli with vagrancy.
Ok er því var lokit, þá mælti Bolli:	And when that was finished, then spoke Bolli:	And when it was over, Bolli said:
"Þú hefir mikit við, Helgi, ok mun betr fallit at leika nökkut í móti við þik".	"You have much with, Helgi, and should better make that sport somewhat in meeting with you".	"You are making a lot of it, Helgi, and it would be better to play something against you".

The Tale of Bolli Bollason (Old Norse)

Old Norse	Literal	English
Þá hefr Bolli upp stefnu ok stefndi Helga um illmæli við sik ok annarri stefnu um brekráð til fjár síns.	Then had Bolli upped summons and charged Helgi about slander with him and another summons about treachery to wealth his.	Then Bolli instituted a summons, and sued Helgi for a slander against him, and another summons for accusations of treachery to his property.
Þeir mæltu, förunautar hans, at drepa skyldi skelmi þann.	There spoke, companions his, that kill should devilish-man then.	They, his companions, said that the scoundrel should be killed.
Bolli kvað þat eigi skyldu.	Bolli said that not should.	Bolli said it was not his duty.
Bolli lét varða skóggang.	Bolli had warranted outlawry.	Bolli had warranted outlawry.
Hann mælti eftir stefnuna:	He spoke after the-summons:	He said after the summons:
"Þér skuluð færa heim húsfreyju Helga kníf ok belti, er ek sendi henni, því at mér er sagt, at hon hafi gott eina lagt til várra haga".	"You should bring home housewife Helgi knife and belt, that I send her, because to me is said, that she had benefit one had to ours fairly".	"You should bring home this knife and belt for your housewife that I send her, because I am told that she spoke up fairly for us".
Bolli ríðr nú í brott, en Helgi er þar eftir.	Bolli rode now to away, then Helgi was there afterwards.	Bolli now rode away, and Helgi was left behind.
Þeir Bolli koma til Þorsteins á Háls ok fá þar góðar viðtökur.	They Bolli came to Thorstein's at Hals and got there good with-taken.	Bolli and his men came to Thorstein at Hals and were well received there.
Er þar búin veizla fríð.	As there prepared feast peaceful.	There was a beautiful feast there.

7

Nú er at segja frá Helga, at hann kemr heim á Skeið ok segir húsfreyju sinni, hvat þeir Bolli höfðu við átzt.	Now is it to-say from Helgi, that he came home at Skeid and told housewife his, what they Bolli had with to.	Now it is said of Helgi that he came home to Skeid and told his housewife what Bolli and they had done.
"Þykkjumst ek eigi vita", segir hann, "hvat mér verðr til ráðs at eiga við slíkan mann sem Bolli er, ne ek em málamaðr engi.	"Think I not know", said he, "what to-me becomes to advice that have with such men as Bolli is, nor I am man-of-law none.	"I do not think I know", he said, "what I can do with such a man as Bolli is, nor am I a lawyer.
Á ek ok ekki marga, þá er mér muni at málum veita".	As I also not many, then that me would to the-matter grant".	I also do not have many who will help me".

The Tale of Bolli Bollason (Old Norse)

Old Norse	Literal	English
Sigríðr húsfreyja svarar:	Sigrid housewife answered:	Sigrid the housewife answered:
"Þú ert orðinn mannfóli mikill, hefir átt við ina göfgustu menn ok gert þik at undri.	"You have become an-idiot much, have had with these noblest men and made you a fool-of-yourself.	"You have been very foolish, you have dealt with these noblest men, and you have made a fool of yourself.
Mun þér ok fara sem makligt er, at þú munt hér fyrir upp gefa allt fé þitt ok sjálfan þik".	Should you also go as deserve then, that you should here because-of up give all wealth yours and yourself you".	It will be as you deserve, that you shall lose your wealth and your life".
Helgi heyrði á orð hennar ok þóttu ill vera, en grunaði þó, at satt myndi vera, því at honum var svá farit, at íhann var vesalmenni ok þó skapillr ok heimskr.	Helgi heard the words hers and thought ill were, but suspected though, that true would be, because that he was so fared, that cowardly was wretch and though bad-temper and foolishness.	Helgi heard her words, and thought they were evil, but still suspected that it would be true, for he had done so, that he was a poor man, and yet temperamental and foolish.
Sá hann sik engi færi hafa til leiðréttu, en mælt sik í ófæru.	Saw he such no way-out had to rectify, what talked himself into impassable.	He saw that he had no opportunity to correct himself, the impasse he had talked himself into.
Barst hann heldr illa af fyrir þetta allt jafnsaman.	Overcome he rather ill of for this all together.	He was overcome badly for all of it all at once.
Sigríðr lét taka sér hest ok reið at finna Þorstein, frænda sinn, Narfason, ok váru þeir Bolli þá komnir.	Sigrid had taken her horse and rode to find Thorstein, kinsman hers, Narfason, and were they Bolli then come.	Sigrid had a horse taken, and rode to find Thorstein, her kinsman, Narfason, and Bolli and his men had arrived.
Hon heimti Þorstein á mál ok sagði honum, í hvert efni komit var.	She asked-for Thorstein to speak-to and told him, about how the-matter come was.	She called Thorstein to speak to and told him what had happened.
"Þó hefir slíkt illa til tekizt", svarar Þorsteinn.	"Though has such ill to taken", answered Thorstein.	This has turned out very badly", answered Thorstein.
Hon sagði ok, hversu vel Bolli hafði boðit eða hversu heimskliga Helga fór.	She told also, how well Bolli had offered an how-so foolishly Helgi did.	She also said how well Bolli had offered and how stupid Helgi was.
Bað hon Þorstein eiga í allan hlut, at þetta mál greiddist.	Asked she Thorstein to-have it all lot, that this matter resolved.	She asked Thorstein to have everything to do with this matter being settled.

The Tale of Bolli Bollason (Old Norse)

Old Norse	Literal	English
Eftir þat fór hon heim, en Þorsteinn kom at máli við Bolla:	After that went she home, and Thorstein came to speak with Bolli:	After that she went home, then Thorstein spoke to Bolli:
"Hvat er um, vinr", segir hann, "hvárt hefir Helgi af Skeiði sýnt fólsku mikla við þik? Vil ek biðja, at þér leggið niðr fyrir mín orð ok virðið þat engis, því at ómæt eru þar afglapa orð".	"What is about, friend", said he, "how has Helgi of Skeid shown falsehood much with you?" Wish I offer, that you lay down for my words and honour that none, therefore that un-good are there foolish words".	"What is the matter, friend?" he said, "has Helgi of Skeid shown great falsehood to you? I want to ask you to lay down those words and do not honour them, because they are foolish words there".
Bolli svarar:	Bolli answered:	Bolli answers:
"Þat er víst, at þetta er engis vert.	"That is certainly, that this is none worthy.	"It is certain that this is of no value.
Mun ek mér ok ekki um þetta gefa".	Should I to-me also not about this give".	I will not worry about this".
"Þá vil ek", sagði Þorsteinn, "at þér gefið honum upp þetta fyrir mína skyld ok hafið þar fyrir mína vináttu".	"Then wish I", said Thorstein, "that you give him up this for my guilt and have there for my friendship".	"Then I wish", said Thorstein, "that you give him this for my sake, and have it there for my friendship".
"Ekki mun þetta til neins váða horfa", sagði Bolli,	"Not would this to any risk turn", said Bolli,	"This will not look to any risk", said Bolli,
"lét ek mér fátt um finnast, ok bíðr þat várdaga".	"let I me few about encounter, and wait to spring-days".	"I did not care much for it, and it will wait for spring days".
Þorsteinn mælti:	Thorstein spoke:	Thorstein said:
"Þat mun ek sýna, at mér þykkir máli skipta, at þetta gangi eftir mínum vilja.	"That would I show, that to-me thought the-matter exchange, that this going after my will.	"I will show that it is important to me that this goes according to my will.
Ek vil gefa þér hest þann, er beztr er hér í sveitum, ok eru tólf saman hrossin".	I will give you horse then, the best is here in the-district, and there twelve together herd".	I want to give you the horse that is the best here in the countryside, and there are twelve horses together".
Bolli svarar:	Bolli answered:	Bolli answers:
"Slíkt er allvel boðit, en eigi þarftu at leggja hér svá mikla stund á.	"Such is all-well offered, but not need-you to have here so much while to.	"Such a thing is very well offered, but you do not have to spend so much time here.
Ek gaf mér lítit um slíkt.	I gave me little about such.	I gave myself little of that.

The Tale of Bolli Bollason (Old Norse)

Old Norse	Literal	English
Mun ok lítit af verða, þá er í dóm kemr".	Should also little of be, then that in self-judgement come".	There will be little of it when it comes to judgment".
"Þat er sannast", sagði Þorsteinn, "at ek vil selja þér sjálfdæmi fyrir málit"	"That is the-truest", said Thorstein, "that I wish repay you self-judgement for the-matter"	"It is true", said Thorstein, "that I wish to grant you self-judgement in this matter".
Bolli svarar:	Bolli answered:	Bolli answered:
"Þat ætla ek sannast, at ekki þurfi um at leitast, því at ek vil ekki sættast á þetta mál".	"That expect I truly, that no need about to seek, because that I wish not reconcile to this case".	"I think it is true that there is no need to seek it, because I do not want to accept a settlement in this matter".
"Þá kýstu þat, er öllum oss gegnir verst", sagði Þorsteinn.	"Then choosing that, which all us serves the-worst", said Thorstein.	"Then you are choosing what is worst for all of us" said Thorstein.
"Þótt Helgi sé lítils verðr, þá er hann þó í venzlum bundinn við oss.	"Though Helgi is little worth, then is he though in marriage bound with us.	"Although Helgi is of little value, he is still bound to us.
Þá munum vér hann eigi upp gefa undir vápn yðor, síðan þú vill engis mín orð virða.	Then should we him not up give into weapons yours, after you wish none my words value.	Then we will not give him up under your weapons, since you do not want to honour my words.
En at þeim atkvæðum, at Helgi hafði í stefnu við þik, lízt mér þat engi sæmðarauki, þó at þat sé á þing borit".	But that them charges, that Helgi has in summoned with you, appears to-me that none honour, though that it is at the-assembly carried".	But with the charges that Helgi had in summons with you, I do not think it is an honour, even though it has been presented to the assembly".
Skilðu þeir Þorsteinn ok Bolli heldr fáliga.	Separated they Thorstein and Bolli rather poorly.	Thorstein and Bolli parted rather poorly.
Ríðr hann í brott ok hans félagar, ok er ekki getit, at hann sé með gjöfum í brott leystr.	Rode he to away and his comrades, and was not got, that he being with gifts in away releasing.	He and his companions rode away, and it is not mentioned that he was released with gifts.

8

Bolli ok hans förunautar kómu á Möðruvöllu til Guðmundar ins ríka.	Bolli and his companions came to Modruvellir to Gudmund the Powerful.	Bolli and his companions came to Modruvellir to Gudmund the Powerful.

The Tale of Bolli Bollason (Old Norse)

Old Norse	Literal	English
Hann gengr í móti þeim með allri blíðu ok var inn glaðasti.	He came to meet them with all joyfulness and was the gladdest.	He came to meet them with all joyfulness and was the gladdest.
Þar sátu þeir hálfan mánuð í góðum fagnaði.	There stayed they half a-month in good celebration.	They stayed there half a-month in good celebration.
Þá mælti Guðmundr til Bolla:	Then spoke Gudmund to Bolli:	Then Gudmund said to Bolli:
"Hvat er til haft um þat, hefir sundrþykki orðit með yðr Þorsteini?"	"What is to have about that, have discord words with your Thorstein?"	"What is that matter, has there been discord with you and Thorstein?"
Bolli kvað lítit til haft um þat ok tók annat mál.	Bolli spoke little to have about that and took another matter.	Bolli said he had little to say about it and took another matter.
Guðmundr mælti:	Gudmund spoke:	Gudmund said:
"Hverja leið ætlar þú aftr at ríða?"	"What way intend you return to ride?"	"Which way are you going to ride back?"
"Ina sömu", svarar Bolli.	"The same", answered Bolli.	"The same", answered Bolli.
Guðmundr mælti:	Gudmund spoke:	Gudmund said:
"Letja vil ek yðr þess, því at mér er svá sagt, at þit Þorsteinn hafið skilit fáliga.	"Discourage wish I you this, because that to-me is so said, that you Thorstein have separated coldly.	"I wish to discourage you, for I am told that Thorstein has separated with you poorly.
Ver heldr hér með mér ok ríð suðr í vár, ok látum þá þessi mál ganga til vegar".	Be rather here with me and ride south in spring, and let then this matter go its way".	Stay here with me and ride south in the spring, and then let these matters go".
Bolli lézt eigi mundu bregða ferðinni fyrir hót þeira, "en þat hugða ek, þá er Helgi fólit lét sem heimskligast ok mælti hvert óorðan at öðru við oss ok vildi hafa spjótit konungsnaut ór hendi mér fyrir einn heyvöndul, at ek skylda freista, at hann fengi ombun orða sinna.	Bolli said not would break travel for threat theirs, "but that think I, then that Helgi foolishly had as foolishly and speaking each slanderous to another with us and willing to-have spear king's-gift out-of hand mine for only a-haystack, that I should test, that he gets return words his.	Bolli said that he would not break from his travel plans because of their threat, "but I think that Helgi was stupid, and spoke foolishly with one slanderous charge after another to us, and wanting to take the spear King's Gift out of my hand for only a haystack, I should see to it that he gets what he deserves for his words.

The Tale of Bolli Bollason (Old Norse)

Old Norse	Literal	English
Hefi ek ok annat ætlat fyrir spjótinu, at ek mynda heldr gefa þér ok þar með gullhringinn, þann er stólkonungrinn gaf mér.	Have I also other plans for spear, that I should rather give to-you and there with gold-ring, then that the-emperor gave me.	I also have other plans for my spear, as I intend to give it to you, along with the gold arm ring that the emperor gave me.
Hygg ek nú, at gripirnir sé betr niðr komnir en þá, at Helgi hefði þá".	Think I now, that treasures are better kinsman coming than then, that Helgi has then".	I think now, that the treasures are better coming to a kinsman than Helgi having them".
Guðmundr þakkaði honum gjafar þessar ok mælti:	Gudmund thanked him the-gift these and spoke:	Gudmund thanked him for these gifts, and said,
"Hér munu smæri gjafar í móti koma en verðugt er".	"Here shall smaller gifts in return coming than worth are".	"Here smaller gifts will come in return than are worthy".
Guðmundr gaf Bolla skjöld gulllagðan ok gullhring ok skikkju.	Gudmund gave Bolli shield gold-laid and gold-ring and cloak.	Gudmund gave Bolli a gold-plated shield and a gold ring and a cloak.
Var í henni it dýrsta klæði ok búin öll, þar er bæta þótti.	Were about her the dearest clothing and prepared all, there was better thought.	And about it was prepared all the most precious material that made it better.
Allir váru gripirnir mjök ágætir.	All were treasures much renowned.	All the treasures were very good.
Þá mælti Guðmundr:	Then spoke Gudmund:	Then Gudmund said:
"Illa þykkir mér þú gera, Bolli, er þú vill ríða um Svarfaðardal".	"Bad think I you doing, Bolli, that you wish to-ride about Svarfadardal".	"I think you do badly, Bolli, when you want to ride through Svarfadardal".
Bolli segir þat ekki skaða munu.	Bolli said that not scathed would-be.	Bolli said that he would not be scathed.
Riðu þeir í brott, ok skilja þeir Guðmundr við inum mestum kærleikum.	Rode they to away, and separated they Gudmund with the most friendship.	They rode away, and Gudmund parted with the greatest friendship.
Þeir Bolli ríða nú veg sinn út um Galmarströnd.	Then Bolli rode now way his out about Galmarstrond.	Then Bolli and his men rode their way out over Galmarstrond.
Um kveldit kómu þeir á þann bæ, er at Krossum heitir.	About evening came they to the farm, which that Krossar named.	In the evening they came to a town called Krossar.
Þar bjó sá maðr, er Óttarr hét.	There lived so a-man, who Ottar named.	There lived a man named Ottar.

The Tale of Bolli Bollason (Old Norse)

Old Norse	Literal	English
Hann stóð úti.	He stood outside.	He stood outside.
Hann var sköllóttr ok í skinnstakki	He was bald and in skin-cloak.	He was bald, and wearing a fur coat.
Óttarr kvaddi þá vel ok bauð þeim þar at vera.	Ottar greeted then well and invited them there to be.	Ottar greeted them well and invited them to stay there.
Þat þiggja þeir.	That accepted they.	They accepted.
Var þar góðr beini ok bóndi inn kátasti.	Were there good benefit and farmer the merriest.	There was a good benefit and the farmer was merry.
Váru þeir þar um nóttina.	Were they there about the-night.	They were there that night.
Um morgininn, er þeir Bolli váru ferðar búnir, þá mælti Óttarr:	About morning, when they Bolli were travel preparing, then spoke Ottar:	In the morning, when Bolli and his men were ready to go, Ottar said:
"Vel hefir þú gert, Bolli, er þú hefir sótt heim bæ minn.	"Well have you done, Bolli, that you have sought home farm mine.	"You have done well, Bolli, when you have visited my farm.
Vil ek ok sýna þér lítit tillæti, gefa þér gullhring ok kunna þökk, at þú þiggir.	Wish I also show you little deference, give you gold-ring and know thanks, that you accept.	I also want to show you a little favour, and give you a gold ring and I would be thankful if you accept.
Hér er ok fingrgull, er fylgja skal".	Here is also gold-ring, that follow shall".	Here is also a gold ring to go with it".
Bolli þiggr gjafarnar ok þakkar bónda.	Bolli accepted the-gifts and thanks the-farmer.	Bolli accepted the gifts and thanked the farmer.
Óttarr var á hesti sínum því næst ok reið fyrir þeim leiðina, því at fallit hafði snjór lítill um nóttina.	Ottar was about horse his as nearest and rode ahead them the-way, because that fallen had snow little about the-night.	Ottar was then on his horse, and rode in front of them, for little snow had fallen that night.
Þeir ríða nú veg sinn út til Svarfaðardals,	They rode now way theirs out to Svarfadardal,	They now rode their way out to Svarfadardal,
ok er þeir hafa eigi lengi riðit, snerist hann við Óttarr ok mælti til Bolla:	and when they had not long ridden, turned he with Ottar and spoke to Bolli:	and when they had not ridden long, Ottar turned to Bolli and said:

The Tale of Bolli Bollason (Old Norse)

Old Norse	Literal	English
"Þat mun ek sýna, at ek vilda, at þú værir vin minn.	"That should I show, that I wish, that you be friend mine.	"I will show that I wish you to be my friend.
Er hér annarr gullhringr, er ek vil þér gefa.	Is here another gold-ring, that I wish to-you to-give.	Here's another gold ring I want to give you.
Væra ek yðr velviljaðr í því, er ek mætta.	Be I your well-willing for accordingly, as I might.	I wish to help you in any way that I might.
Munuð þér ok þess þurfa".	Shall you also this need".	If you shall need it".
Bolli kvað bónda fara stórmannliga til sín, "en þó vil ek þiggja hringinn".	Bolli thanked the-farmer going great-man-ness to him, "but though wish I to-accept the-ring".	Bolli thanked the farmer for being so generous, "but still I want to accept the ring".
"Þá gerir þú vel", segir bóndi.	"Then doing you well", said the-farmer.	"Then you do well", said the farmer.

9

Nú er at segja frá Þorsteini af Hálsi.	Now is to say from Thorstein of Hals.	Now the story turns to Thorstein of Hals.
Þegar honum þykkir ván, at Bolli muni norðan ríða, þá safnar hann mönnum ok ætlar at sitja fyrir Bolla ok vill nú, at verði umskipti um mál þeira Helga.	When he thought expected, that Bolli would north ride, then collected he men and intended to sit-in-ambush before Bolli and wishing now, to become about-exchanged about the-matter theirs Helgi.	When he expected Bolli to ride north, he gathered men and intended to sit in ambush before Bolli, and now wished to alter the matter between him and Helgi.
Þeir Þorsteinn hafa þrjá tigu manna ok ríða fram til Svarfaðardalsár ok setjast þar.	They Thorstein had three ten men and rode from to Svarfadardal and stayed there.	Thorstein and his men had thirty men, and rode up to Svarfadardal, and settled there.
Ljótr hét maðr, er bjó á Völlum í Svarfaðardal.	Ljot was-named a-man, who lived at Vellir in Svarfadardal.	There was a man named Ljot, who lived at Vellir in Svarfadardal.
Hann var höfðingi mikill ok vinsæll ok málamaðr mikill.	He was chieftain great and popular and law-man great.	He was a great chieftain, popular, and a great man of law.

The Tale of Bolli Bollason (Old Norse)

Old Norse	Literal	English
Þat var búningr hans hversdagliga, at hann hafði svartan kyrtil ok refði í hendi, en ef hann bjóst til víga, þá hafði hann blán kyrtil ok öxi snaghyrnda.	It was costume his everyday, that he had a-black tunic and poleaxe in hand, but if he prepared to fight, then had he a-blue tunic and axe snag-cornered.	It was his everyday costume that he had a black tunic and a poleaxe in his hand, but if he was preparing for battle, he had a blue tunic and a sharp-edged axe.
Var hann þá heldr ófrýnligr.	Was he then rather inconspicuous.	He was then rather inconspicuous.
Þeir Bolli ríða út eftir Svarfaðardal.	They Bolli rode out along Svarfadardal.	Bolli and his men rode out along Svarfadardal.
Fylgir Óttarr þeim út um bæinn at Hálsi ok at ánni út.	Followed Ottar them out about the-farm at Hals and to-the-river from.	Ottar followed them out of the town at Hals and out to the river.
Þar sat fyrir þeim Þorsteinn við sína menn, ok þegar er Óttarr sér fyrirsátina, bregðr hann við ok keyrir hest sinn þvers í brott.	There sat before them Thorstein with his men, and when that Ottar saw for-the-ambush, broke he with and spurred horse his across to away.	There Thorstein sat before them with his men, and when Ottar saw the ambush, he responded and drove his horse across.
Þeir Bolli ríða at djarfliga, ok er þeir Þorsteinn sjá þat ok hans menn, spretta þeir upp.	They Bolli rode to boldly, and when they Thorstein saw that and his men, sprang they up.	Bolli and his men rode boldly, and when Thorstein and his men saw it, they sprang up.
Þeir váru sínum megin ár hvárir, en áin var leyst með löndum, en íss flaut á miðri.	There were they sides the-river opposite, about the-river was down with land, was ice floating in the-middle.	They were on either side of the river, but the river flowed with land, and ice floated in the middle.
Hleypa þeir Þorsteinn út á ísinn.	Ran they Thorstein out into the-ice.	Thorstein and his men ran out onto the ice.
Helgi af Skeiði var ok þar ok eggjar þá fast ok kvað nú vel, at þeir Bolli reyndi, hvárt honum væri kapp sitt ok metnaðr einhlítt eða hvárt nökkurir menn norðr þar myndi þora at halda til móts við hann.	Helgi of Skeid was also there and encouraged then closely and said now well, that they Bolli test, whether he was eager his and pride unanimously or whether some men north there would dare to hold to meet with him.	Helgi of Skeid was also there and encouraged them, and said that Bolli and his men would be tested as to whether he was eagerness and pride would be unanimous, or whether there were men of the north who would dare to meet him.
"Þarf nú ok eigi at spara at drepa þá alla.	"Need now and not that spare to kill then all.	"We do not need to spare from killing them all.

The Tale of Bolli Bollason (Old Norse)

Old Norse	Literal	English
Mun þat ok leiða öðrum", sagði Helgi, "at veita oss ágang".	Would it also loath others", said Helgi, "that giving us aggression".	As it would also deter others", said Helgi, "from attacking us".
Bolli heyrir orð Helga ok sér, hvar hann er kominn út á ísinn.	Bolli heard words Helgi's and saw, where he had come out on the-ice.	Bolli heard Helgi's words and saw where he had come out on the ice.
Bolli skýtr at honum spjóti, ok kemr á hann miðjan.	Bolli shot at him spear, and came it his middle.	Bolli shot at him with a spear, and struck him in the middle.
Fellr hann á bak aftr í ána, en spjótit flýgr í bakkann öðrum megum, svá at fast var, ok hekk Helgi þar á niðr í ána.	Fell he on back back in river, but the-spear followed the bank other may, so that fastened was, and hung Helgi there at down in the-river.	He fell backwards into the river, but the spear flew into the bank the other way, so that it was stuck, and Helgi hung down there in the river.
Eftir þat tókst þar bardagi inn skarpasti.	After that took there battle the hardest.	After that, the battle became the hardest.
Bolli gengr at svá fast, at þeir hrökkva undan, er nær váru.	Bolli went to so fast, that they recoiled away-from, who near were.	Bolli went so fast that those who were near him recoiled.
Þá sótti fram Þorsteinn í móti Bolla, ok þegar þeir fundust, höggr Bolli til Þorsteins á öxlina, ok varð þat mikit sár.	Then sought from Thorstein to meet Bolli, and then they found, striking Bolli to Thorstein's with an-axe, and became that much wounding.	Then Thorstein went out to meet Bolli, and when they met, Bolli struck Thorstein on the shoulder, and it was a great wound.
Annat sár fekk Þorsteinn á fæti.	Another wound got Thorstein about the-leg.	Thorstein received another wound on his leg.
Sóknin var in harðasta.	The-struggle was the hardest.	The attack was the hardest.
Bolli varð ok sárr nökkut ok þó ekki mjök.	Bolli became also wounded somewhat and though not much.	Bolli was also slightly injured, but not very badly.
Nú er at segja frá Óttari.	Now is to say from Ottar.	Now the story turns to Ottar.
Hann ríðr upp á Völlu til Ljóts, ok þegar þeir finnast, mælti Óttarr:	He rode up to Vellir to Ljot, and then they met, spoke Ottar:	He rode up to Vellir, to Ljot, and when they met Ottar spoke:
"Eigi er nú setuefni, Ljótr", sagði hann, "ok fylg þú nú virðing þinni, er þér liggr laus fyrir".	"Not is now sitting, Ljot", said he, "and follows you now honour yours, that you lay less for".	"No cause to sit about, Ljot", he said, "what follows now is your honour to prove".

The Tale of Bolli Bollason (Old Norse)

Old Norse	Literal	English
"Hvat er nú helzt í því, Óttarr?"	"What is now rather that according, Ottar?"	"What would that involve, Ottar?"
"Ek hygg, at þeir berist hér niðri við ána Þorsteinn á Hálsi ok Bolli, ok er þat in mesta hamingja at skirra vandræðum þeira".	"I think, that they fight here down by the-river Thorstein of Hals and Bolli, and is that the most fortunate that prevent trouble theirs".	"I expect that they will be fighting here down by the river, Thorstein of Hals and Bolli, and it would be most fortunate to prevent their hostilities".
Ljótr mælti:	Ljot spoke:	Ljot spoke:
"Oft sýnir þú af þér mikinn drengskap".	"Often showed you of your great honour".	"You have often showed great honour".
Ljótr brá við skjótt ok við nökkura menn ok þeir Óttarr báðir.	Ljot startled with quickly and with several men and they Ottar both.	He reacted quickly and with several others hurried back to Ottar.
Ok er þeir koma til árinnar, berjast þeir Bolli sem óðast.	And when they came to the-river, fought they Bolli as furious.	And when they came to the river, Bolli and the others were fighting furiously.
Váru þá fallnir þrír menn af Þorsteini.	Were they fallen three men of Thorstein's.	There were three of Thorstein's men that had fallen.
Þeir Ljótr ganga fram í meðal þeira snarliga, svá at þeir máttu nær ekki at hafast.	Then Ljot went from to between them quickly, so that they may close not to have.	Ljot and his men quickly ran between the fighters so that they could not get close.
Þá mælti Ljótr:	Then spoke Ljot:	Then Ljot spoke:
"Þér skuluð skilja þegar í stað", segir hann, "ok er þó nú ærit at orðit.	"You should separate immediately this place", said he, "and is though now plenty-of has become.	"You should separate immediately from this place", he said, "and now more than enough has been done.
Vil ek einn gera milli yðvar um þessi mál, en ef því níta aðrir hvárir, þá skulum vér veita þeim atgöngu".	Wish I alone to-do between you about this matter, that if therefore refuse others each, then should we grant them to-going".	I alone wish to decide to settle this matter, and if either of you refuses, then they shall be granted an attack".
En með því at Ljótr gekk at svá fast, þá hættu þeir at berjast, ok því játtu hvárirtveggju, at Ljótr skyldi gera um þetta þeira í milli.	Then with because that Ljot went that so close, then stop they the fight, and therefore agreed either-side, that Ljot should do about that their in between.	Then because Ljot went so close, they stopped fighting, and either side agreed, that Ljot should handle the matter between them.

The Tale of Bolli Bollason (Old Norse)

Old Norse	Literal	English
Skilðust þeir við svá búit.	Separated they with so prepared.	They parted ways so prepared.
Fór Þorsteinn heim, en Ljótr býðr þeim Bolla heim með sér, ok þat þiggr hann.	Went Thorstein home, and Ljot invited them Bolli home with him, and that accepted he.	Thorstein went home, but Ljot invited Bolli and his men home with him, and he accepted.
Fóru þeir Bolli á Völlu til Ljóts.	Went they Bolli to Vellir to Ljot's.	Bolli and his men went to Vellir to Ljot's.
Þar heitir í Hestanesi, sem þeir höfðu barizt.	There named is Hestanes, which they had bears.	There is named Hestanes, which bears today.
Óttarr bóndi skilðist eigi fyrri við þá Bolla en þeir kómu heim með Ljóti.	Ottar the-farmer separated not before with then Bolli then they came home with Ljot.	Farmer Ottar did not part with Bolli until they came home with Ljot.
Gaf Bolli honum stórmannligar gjafar at skilnaði ok þakkaði honum vel sitt liðsinni.	Gave Bolli him great-man-like gifts as parted and thanked him well this assistance.	Bolli gave him great gifts at parting, and thanked him well for his help.
Hét Bolli Óttari sinni vináttu.	Pledged Bolli Ottar his friendship.	Bolli pledged Ottar his friendship.
Fór hann heim til Krossa ok sat í búi sínu.	Travelled he home to Krossar and stayed in farm his.	He went home to Krossar and stayed at his farm.

10

Eftir bardagann í Hestanesi fór Bolli heim með Ljóti á Völlu við alla sína menn, en Ljótr bindr sár þeira, ok greru þau skjótt, því at gaumr var at gefinn.	After the-battle at Hestanes travelled Bolli home with Ljot to Vellir with all his men, then Ljot bound wounds theirs, and healed they quickly, because that attention were for given.	After the battle in Hestanes, Bolli went home with Ljot at Vellir with all his men, where Ljot bound up their wounds, and they healed quickly, for the attention was paid to them.
En er þeir váru heilir sára sinna, þá stefndi Ljótr þing fjölmennt.	Then when they were safe wounds theirs, then summoned Ljot assembly full-of-people.	Then when they were healed of their wounds, Ljot convened a great assembly.
Riðu þeir Bolli á þingit.	Rode they Bolli to the-assembly.	Bolli and his men rode to the assembly.
Þar kom ok Þorsteinn af Hálsi við sína menn.	There came also Thorstein of Hals with his men.	Thorstein of Hals also came there with his men.

The Tale of Bolli Bollason (Old Norse)

Old Norse	Literal	English
Ok er þingit var sett, mælti Ljótr:	And when the-assembly was set, spoke Ljot:	And when the Thing was set, Ljot said,
"Nú skal ekki fresta uppsögn um gerð þá, er ek hefi samit milli þeira Þorsteins af Hálsi ok Bolla.	"Now shall not postpone up-saying about made then, but I have agreement between they Thorstein's of Hals and Bolli.	"Now the conclusion of the agreement which I have brought up between Thorstein of Hals and Bolli shall not be postponed.
Hefi ek þat upphaf at gerðinni, at Helgi skal hafa fallit óheilagr fyrir illyrði sín ok tiltekju við Bolla.	Have I that begun to make, that Helgi shall have failed unholy for ill-words his and exchange with Bolli.	I have the beginning of the deed, that Helgi has fallen without right for compensation for his wickedness and betrayal of Bolli.
Sárum þeira Þorsteins ok Bolla jafna ek saman,	The-wounds they Thorstein's and Bolli equal I the-same,	I will make amends for the wounds of Thorstein and Bolli,
en þeir þrír menn, er fellu af Þorsteini, skal Bolli bæta.	But they three men who fell of Thorstein shall Bolli compensate.	but the three men who fell from Thorstein shall be compensated by Bolli.
En fyrir fjörráð við Bolla ok fyrirsát skal Þorsteinn greiða honum fimmtán hundruð þriggja alna aura.	But for plotting-against with Bolli and ambush shall Thorstein assist him fifteen hundred three ells pay.	But for the conspiracy and plotting-against Bolli, Thorstein shall pay him fifteen hundred three cubit lengths of homespun cloth.
Skulu þeir at þessu alsáttir".	Shall they at this all-settle".	They shall all settle at this".
Eftir þat var slitit þinginu.	After it was dissolved the-assembly.	After that the assembly was dissolved.
Segir Bolli Ljóti, at hann mun ríða heimleiðis, ok þakkar honum vel alla sína liðveizlu, ok skiptust þeir fögrum gjöfum við ok skilðu við góðum vinskap.	Told Bolli Ljot, that he would ride home-ways, and thanked him well all his assistance, and exchanged they fair gifts with and separated with good friendship.	Bolli told Ljot that he would ride home, and thanked him well for all his help, and they exchanged beautiful gifts and parted with good friendship.
Bolli tók upp bú Sigríðar á Skeiði, því at hon vildi fara vestr með honum.	Bolli took up the-farm Sigrid of Skeid, because that she wished to-travel west with him.	Bolli took up Sigrid's estate at Skeid, because she wanted to go west with him.
Ríða þau veg sinn, þar til er þau koma á Miklabæ til Arnórs.	Rode they way theirs, there until that they came to Miklabaer to Arnor's.	They rode their way, until they came to Miklabær to Arnor.
Tók hann harðla vel við þeim,	Took he greatly well with them,	He received them very kindly,

The Tale of Bolli Bollason (Old Norse)

Old Norse	Literal	English
dvölðust þar um hríð, ok sagði Bolli Arnóri allt um skipti þeira Svarfdæla, hversu farit hafði.	dwelled there about awhile, and told Bolli Arnor all about exchanged theirs Svarfadardal, how-so gone had.	they stayed there for a while, and Bolli told Arnor all about the exchange of the Svarfadardal, and how things had gone.
Arnórr mælti:	Arnor spoke:	Arnor said:
"Mikla heill hefir þú til borit um ferð þessa, við slíkan mann sem þú áttir, þar er Þorsteinn var.	"Much luck have you to bear about journey this, with such a-man as you have, there as Thorstein was.	"You have been very lucky in this journey, and in your dealings with such a man as Thorstein.
Er þat sannast um at tala, at fáir eða engir höfðingjar munu sótt hafa meira frama ór öðrum heruðum norðr hingat en þú, þeir sem jafnmarga öfundarmenn áttu hér fyrir".	Is it true about that said, that few or none chieftains should attend have more honour of other provinces north here than you, they who equal-many slanderous-men had here for".	Is it true to say that few or no chiefs will have sought more fame from other provinces north here than you, those who had so many envious people here before".
Bolli ríðr nú í brott af Miklabæ við sína menn ok heim suðr.	Bolli rode now to away from Miklabaer with his men and home south.	Bolli now rode away from Miklabær with his men and home south.
Tala þeir Arnórr til vináttu með sér af nýju at skilnaði.	Spoke they Arnor to friendship with them of anew at parting.	Bolli and Arnor spoke of friendship anew before parting.
En er Bolli kom heim í Tungu, varð Þórdís, húsfreyja hans, honum fegin.	Then when Bolli came home to Tunga, was Thordis, housewife his, to-him relieved.	But when Bolli came home to Tunga, Thordis, his housewife, was glad to see him.
Hafði hon frétt áðr nökkut af róstum þeira Norðlendinga ok þótti mikit í hættu, at honum tækist vel til.	Had she news before some of unruliness theirs The-northerners and thought much at danger, that he took well to.	She had heard something before about the skirmishes of the Northerners, and thought it was very dangerous for him to succeed.
Sitr Bolli nú í búi sínu með mikilli virðingu.	Stayed Bolli now at farm his with much honour.	Bolli now stayed in his estate with great honour.
Þessi ferð Bolla var ger at nýjum sögum um allar sveitir, ok töluðu allir einn veg um, at slík þótti varla farin hafa verit náliga.	This journey Bolli's was made to new sagas about all areas, and told all one way about, that such thought barely gone had been near-to.	This journey of Bolli was the subject of new stories about all the districts, and everyone agreed that such a thing was scarcely thought to have been equalled.
Óx virðing hans af slíku ok mörgu öðru.	Grew respect his of such and many others.	His respect from this and many other things grew.

The Tale of Bolli Bollason (Old Norse)

Old Norse	Literal	English
Bolli fekk Sigríði gjaforð göfugt ok lauk vel við hana,	Bolli found Sigrid married worthy and concluded well with her,	Bolli gave Sigrid a noble marriage match and it concluded well,
ok höfum vér eigi heyrt þessa sögu lengri.	and have we none heard this saga longer.	and we have not heard any more of this story.

The Tale of Bolli Bollason (Old Norse)

Word List *(Old Norse to English)*

Old Norse	English

A, a

Old Norse	English
aðra	another
aðrir	others
af	from, from, of, of, off, to
afglapa	foolish
afréttum	the-pastures
aftr	back, down, return, returned
albúnir	all-prepared
aldri	age, never
alizt	homes
alla	all, all
allan	all
allar	all
allir	all, all
allra	of-all
allri	all
alls	all
allstórmannliga	all-great-man-like
allt	all, all
allvel	all-well, all-well
alna	ells
alsáttir	all-settle
alþingi	the-assembly
andvirki	haystacks
annarr	another
annarri	another
annat	another, other
Arnóri	Arnor (name)
Arnórr	Arnor (name)
Arnórs	Arnor's (name)
at	a, about, as, at, for, from, has, have, in, it, of, that, the, to
atgöngu	to-going
atkvæðum	charges
auðigr	rich
aura	pay

Á, á

Old Norse	English
á	about, as, at, for, from, in, into, it, of, on, the, to, up, was, with
áðr	before, earlier
áðu	to
ágætir	renowned
ágætliga	greatly
ágang	aggression
áin	the-river
ána	river, the-river, the-river
ánni	the-river
ár	the-river
árinnar	the-river
ásjá	assistance
áskorun	challenge
átján	eighteen
átt	had
átta	eight
átti	had, married
áttir	have
áttu	had, have-you
átzt	to

Æ, æ

Old Norse	English
æðimaðr	frenzy-man
æja	rest
ærin	considerable
ærit	plenty-of
ætla	expect, intend, intended
ætlar	intend, intended
ætlat	intended, plans
ættsmár	of-family-small

Word List (Old Norse to English)

Old Norse	English

B, b

bað	asked, ordered
báðir	both
bæ	a-farm, farm
bæinn	the-farm
bænum	farmhouse, the-farm
bæta	better, compensate
bak	back
baki	horseback
bakkann	bank
bardagann	the-battle
bardagi	battle
barizt	bears
barst	overcome
bauð	invited
beiða	offer
beiðast	ask
beiddi	asked
beini	benefit
belti	belt
berist	fight
berjast	fight, fought
berr	bear
betr	better
betra	better
betri	better
bezt	best
bezta	best
beztr	best
biðja	offer
bíðr	wait
bindr	bound
Bjarnar	Bjarni (name)
bjó	lived
bjóða	offer, to-invite
bjóst	prepared
bjuggu	lived
blán	a-blue
blári	black
blíðu	joyfulness
blika	shining
boðit	bid, offered
boli	the-bull
Bolla	Bolli (name), Bolli's (name)
Bollason	Bollason (name), Son-of-Bolli (name)
Bollasyni	Bollason (name)
Bolli	Bolli (name)
bónda	husband, the-farmer
bóndi	farmer, host, the-farmer
borit	bear, carried
börnum	children
brá	startled
bræðr	brothers
bræðra	the-brothers
braut	broke
bregða	break
bregðr	broke, drew
brekráð	treachery
bróðir	brother
bróður	brother
brosti	laughed
brotit	broken
brott	away
bú	the-farm
búa	settlers
búast	prepare
búðardurunum	the-booth-doors
búðina	the-booth
búi	farm
búin	prepared
búit	prepared
bundinn	bound
búningr	costume
búnir	preparing
býðr	invited
býr	prepared
býst	prepared

D, d

dauðr	dead
desjarnar	the-hay
djarfliga	boldly
Dögurðarnes	Dagverdarnes (place)
dóm	self-judgement

Word List (Old Norse to English)

Old Norse	English
dregr	drew
drengiligsta	bravely
drengskap	honour
drepa	kill
drepit	kill, killing
dvölðust	dwelled
dýrsta	dearest

E, e

Old Norse	English
eða	an, and, or
ef	if
efni	matter, the-matter
efniligastr	promising
eftir	after, afterwards, along
eftirmálinu	the-after-matter
eftirmáls	after-matter
eggjar	encouraged
eiga	have, in, to-have
eigi	no, none, not
eign	own
eigna	own
eina	one
einhlítt	unanimously
einhvern	one
einir	only
einn	alone, one, only
einsætt	one-agreement
einum	any
ek	I
ekki	no, not, nothing
em	am
en	about, and, but, in, since, than, that, then, was, what, whether
enga	none
engi	no, none
engir	none
engis	none
engrar	no, none
engu	nothing
enn	but, the, then
er	am, and, are, as, but, had, is, it-is, that, the, then, was, were, when, which, who
erfit	difficulty
ert	have
ertu	are-you
eru	are, are-there, is, there, were
eruð	are
eyða	devastate

F, f

Old Norse	English
fá	fee, got
fær	accomplished, got, travelled
færa	bring, bringing
færi	travel, way-out
fæti	the-leg
fagnaði	celebration
fagnat	welcomed
fáir	few
fáliga	coldly, poorly
fallit	failed, fallen, make
fallnir	fallen
fangi	arms
fann	found
fár	few
fara	go, going, to-travel, travel
fararskjóta	horses
farið	travel
farin	gone
farinn	travelling
farit	fared, gone, travelled
fast	close, closely, fast, fastened
fátt	few
fé	cattle, fee, wealth
fébótum	compensation
fegin	relieved
fekk	found, got
félagar	comrades
félagsskap	comradeship
felldr	falling

Word List (Old Norse to English)

Old Norse	English
fellr	fell
fellu	well
fengi	gets
ferð	journey, travel, travelling
ferðar	travel
ferðina	going
ferðinni	the-journey, travel
ferðir	journey
ferr	goes, going, set-out, travel, travelled, travels
fimmtán	fifteen
fingrgull	gold-ring
finna	find
finnast	encounter, met
finnim	find
fjandskap	fiendship
fjár	of-wealth, wealth
fjarri	far-away
fjölmenna	following-men, many-men
fjölmenni	followers-many
fjölmennt	full-of-people
fjórðungi	district
fjörráð	plotting, plotting-against
fláráðum	treacherous
flaut	floating
fleiri	more
flokk	flock
flýgr	followed
flytir	with-fleetness
fögrum	fair
fólit	foolishly
fólsku	false, falsehood
fór	did, goes, travelled, went
fórtu	travelled-you
fóru	travelled, went
förum	a-journey
förunautar	companions, companions
Fótbít	Leg-Biter (name)
frá	from
frægðarverk	famous-work
frænda	kinsman
frændkona	kinswoman
frændkonu	kinswoman
fram	from
frama	honour, honour
framar	honour
freista	test, try
fresta	postpone
frétt	news
frétti	asking, learned
fréttist	reported
fréttust	reported
fríð	peaceful
fritt	safe
fund	meet
fundr	a-meeting
fundust	found, met
fylg	follows
fylgi	follows
fylgir	followed
fylgja	follow
fylgt	followed
fyrir	ahead, because-of, before, for
fyrirsát	ambush
fyrirsátina	for-the-ambush
fyrr	before
fyrri	before
fyrrum	before-us

G, g

Old Norse	English
gaf	gave
gáfu	gave
Galmarströnd	Galmarstrond (place)
ganga	go, went
gangi	going
gaumr	attention
gefa	give, to-give
gefið	give
gefinn	given
gegnir	serves
gegnum	through
gekk	went
gengit	gone
gengr	came, went

Word List (Old Norse to English)

Old Norse	English
gengu	went
ger	made
gera	do, doing, to-do
gerð	made
gerði	did, made
gerðinni	make
gerðu	did, made
gerið	do
gerir	do, doing
gert	done, made
getit	got
getr	got
giftuvænligr	luck-promised
gjafar	gifts, the-gift
gjafarnar	the-gifts
gjaforð	married
gjalda	pay
gjöfum	gifts
glaðasti	gladdest
gnótt	an-abundance
góða	good
góðar	good
góðr	good
góðum	good
göfgustu	noblest
göfugt	worthy
gott	benefit
graðung	a-bull, bull
graðungr	bull
graðungrinn	the-bull
grán	grey
greiða	assist
greiddist	resolved
greru	healed
grípa	grab
gripirnir	treasures
grjóti	rocks
grunaði	suspected
grunr	suspect
guðdala-starra	Starri-of-Guddalir
Guðdölum	Guddalir (place)
Guðmundar	Gudmund (name)
Guðmundr	Gudmund (name)
Guðrún	Gudrun (name)
gullhring	gold-ring
gullhringinn	gold-ring
gullhringr	gold-ring
gulllagðan	gold-laid
gullrekna	gold-inlaid
gyrðr	buckled

H, h

Old Norse	English
hæðilig	mockery
hægligt	easily
hægt	possible
hættu	danger, stop
haf	have
hafa	had, have, to-have
hafast	have
hafði	had, has
hafi	had
hafið	have
hafir	have
haft	had, have
haga	fairly
halda	hold
haldinn	holds
hálfan	half
hálfsmánaðar	half-month's
hallaði	turned
Háls	Hals (place)
Hálsi	Hals (place)
hamingja	fortunate, luck
hana	he, her
hann	he, him, his
hans	him, his
harðasta	hardest
harðla	greatly
harmaði	mourned
heðan	from-here
heðra	district
hefði	has
hefi	have
hefir	had, has, have
hefr	had
Hegranessþingi	Hegranes (place)-Assembly
Hegranessþings	Hegranes (place)-Assembly

Word List (Old Norse to English)

Old Norse	English
heiðina	the-heath
heilir	safe
heill	luck
heim	home
heima	home
heiman	at-home, from-home
heimanferð	from-home-travel
heimboðanna	home-invitation
heimboðum	home-invitations
heimleiðis	home-ways
heimskliga	foolishly
heimskligast	foolishly
heimskr	foolishness
heimsótt	home-sought
heimti	asked-for
heimul	have-right
heitaðist	called
heiti	am-named
heitinn	named
heitir	named
hekk	hung
heldr	behind, rather
Helga	Helgi (name), Helgi's (name)
Helgi	Helgi (name)
Heljardalsheiði	Heljardal Heath (place)
Hellu-Narfa	Hellu-Narfi (name)
Hellu-Narfasonar	Hellu-Narfason (name)
helt	held
helzt	rather
hendi	hand
hendr	hand
hennar	hers
henni	her
hér	here
heraði	district
heruð	district
heruðum	provinces
hest	horse
hesta	horses
hestana	horses, the-horses
Hestanesi	Hestanes (place)
hesti	horse
hestsins	horse's

Old Norse	English
hét	named, pledged, promised, was-named
hey	hay, hey
heygarð	hay-stacks
heygjöfinni	hay-giving
heyinu	the-hay
heyjum	hay
heyrði	heard
heyrir	heard
heyrt	heard
heyvöndul	a-haystack, hay-bundle
hingat	here
hinu	the
hitt	find
hitti	met
hittir	met
hittust	met
hjá	beside
hjálm	helmet
Hjaltadal	Hjaltadal (place)
Hjaltasona	Hjaltasons (name)
Hjaltasonu	Hjaltasons (name)
Hjaltasynir	Hjaltasons (name), Sons-of-Hjalti (name)
Hjarðarholti	Hjardarholt (place)
hlaupi	running
hleypa	ran
hleypr	ran
hlið	side
hliðhollir	open-whole
hlíðinni	the-slope
hljóp	leapt, ran
hljópu	ran
hljótum	we-get
hlut	lot
hlutir	things
hóf	began
Höfða	Hofdi (place)
höfðingi	chieftain
höfðingjar	chieftains
höfðu	had
Hofi	Hof (place)
Hofs	Hof (place)
höfuð	head
höfum	has, have

Word List (Old Norse to English)

Old Norse	English
höggr	striking
holinu	hollow
hon	she
hönd	hand
höndum	hand, his-hands
honum	he, him, his, to-him
horfa	turn
horfist	looks
horn	horn
hót	threat
hríð	awhile
hringinn	the-ring
hrökkva	recoiled
hrossin	herd
Hrútafirði	Hrutafjord (place)
Hrútafjarðar	Hrutafjord (place)
húðfat	bed-roll
hugða	think
hugðu	thought
hugðum	think
hugsar	thought
hundruð	hundred
hús	a-house
húsfreyja	housewife
húsfreyju	housewife
hválfinu	half
hvar	what, where
hvarf	broke-away
hvárir	each, opposite
hvárirtveggju	either-side
hvárt	how, whether
hvat	what
hverfa	turn
hverfið	turn
hvergi	neither
hverir	who
hverja	what
hverju	every
hvern	what
hverr	who
hversdagliga	everyday
hversu	how, how-so
hvert	each, how, what, which
hvítr	white
hygg	think
hyggja	think

I, i

Old Norse	English
ill	ill
illa	bad, ill
illmæli	slander
illt	bad-terms, ill
illu	evil
illyrði	ill-words
in	the
ina	the, these
inn	inside, the
innan	inside
ins	the
inum	the
it	the

Í, í

Old Norse	English
í	about, at, for, in, into, is, it, on, that, the, this, to
íhann	cowardly
íhlutunarsamr	in-sharing-together
ísinn	the-ice
íss	ice

J, j

Old Norse	English
jafna	equal
jafnan	usually
jafnmarga	equal-many
jafnsaman	together
jarðhús	earth-house
járna	iron-shod
játtu	agreed
Jól	Yule (name)
jörð	earth, the-earth

Word List (Old Norse to English)

Old Norse	English
\[heading\]	

K, k

Old Norse	English
kærleik	friendship
kalla	declare
kallaðr	called
kapp	eager
kappi	warriors
kápu	cape
kasta	cast
kátasti	merriest
kaupmenn	trading-men
kaupmönnum	trading-men
kemr	came, come, coming
Kerlingarnef	Crone's-Nose (name)
keyrði	spurred
keyrir	spurred
klæði	clothing
klaufir	hooves
kníf	knife
kom	came, come
koma	came, coming
komim	come
kominn	came, come
komir	come
komit	came, come
komnir	come, coming
kómu	came
kona	wife, wife-of
konu	wife
konungsnaut	king's-gift
kostr	chose
Krossa	Krossar (place)
Krossum	Krossar (place)
kunna	know
kvað	said, spoke, thanked
kvaddi	greeted
kveddi	greeting
kveldit	evening
kvista	trim
kyrrt	peace, still
kyrtil	tunic
kýstu	choosing

L, l

Old Norse	English
lætr	had
lagði	became, lunged
lagðr	laid
lagt	had
láta	allow, leave
látum	let
laug	bathe
lauk	concluded
launmaðrinn	the-unseen-man
laus	less
leggið	lay
leggja	have, lay
leggr	lunged
leið	journey, passed, way
leiða	loath
leiðina	the-way
leiðréttu	rectify
leik	game
leika	sport
leikim	sport
leit	saw
leita	look, seek
leitast	seek
lengi	long
lengr	any-longer
lengri	longer
lét	had, let
léti	let
letja	discourage
letjast	dissuaded
létti	relieved
léttu	relieved
létu	led, let
leyst	down, solved
leystr	releasing
lézt	said
liðfæri	company-less
líðr	passed
liðsafla	company-provided
liðsinnaðr	team-minded
liðsinni	assistance
liðveizlu	assistance
liggr	lay

Word List (Old Norse to English)

Old Norse	English
líta	look
lítill	little
lítils	little
lítinn	a-little
lítit	little
litlu	little
litu	looked
lízt	appears
Ljóti	Ljot (name), Ljot (place)
Ljótr	Ljot (name)
Ljóts	Ljot (place), Ljot's (name)
lögum	law
lokit	finished
löndum	land
lýsa	describe, show
lýst	shown

M, m

Old Norse	English
má	may
maðr	a-man, man
maðrinn	the-man
mælt	talked
mælti	speaking, spoke
mæltu	spoke
mæta	meet
mætta	might
mætti	may
mágsemð	in-laws
mágsemðar	as-in-laws
makligt	deserve
mál	case, matter, speak-to, the-matter
málamaðr	law-man, man-of-law
máli	discuss, matter, speak, the-matter
málinu	the-case
málit	the-case, the-matter
málóði	of-violent-language
málum	the-matter
mann	a-man, men
manna	men, people's
mannfóli	an-idiot
manni	a-man, man
manninn	person
mannsins	the-man
mánuð	a-month
Marbæli	Marbaeli (place)
Marbælinga	Marbaeli (place)
marga	many
margt	many, much
marki	a-sign
máttu	may
með	with
meðal	between
mega	may
megi	may
megin	sides
megum	may
meiddi	wounded
mein	harm
meir	more
meira	more
meiri	the-more
menn	men, people
mér	for-me, I, me, mine, to-me
merkr	marks
mest	most
mesta	most
mestum	most
metast	meet
metnaðr	pride
miðjan	middle
miðri	the-middle
mik	me, mine, much, my
mikill	great, much
mikilli	much
mikinn	great, much
mikit	much
mikla	much
Miklabæ	Miklabaer (place)
miklir	great
miklu	much
miklum	much
milli	between
mín	mine, my
mína	mine, my
minn	mine

Word List (Old Norse to English)

Old Norse	English
minna	mine
minni	diminish, less
mínum	mine, my
mitt	mine
mjök	great, many, much
Möðruvöllu	Modruvellir (place)
mönnum	men, people, to-people
morgininn	morning
mörgu	many
mót	meeting
móti	meet, return
móts	meet
mun	shall, should, would
muna	should
mund	about-that-time
mundu	would
muni	should, would
munt	should
muntu	shall-you, should-you
munu	shall, should, would, would-be
munuð	shall
munum	shall, should
mynda	should
myndi	should, would

N, n

Old Norse	English
ná	obtain
nær	close, near, when
næst	nearest
nætr	nights
nafn	name, name
náliga	near-to
Narfason	Narfason (name)
náskyld	closely-related
nauðsyn	necessity
nauðsynja	deed-refuse
ne	nor
neins	any
nenni	care
níðingsverk	lowly-deed
niðr	down, kinsman
niðri	down
níta	refuse
nökkura	any, several, somewhat
nökkurir	some
nökkurr	somewhat
nökkut	some, something, somewhat
norðan	north
norðlendinga	the-northerners
norðlendingum	northerners
norðr	north
nóttina	the-night
nú	now
nýju	anew
nýjum	new

O, o

Old Norse	English
ofan	down
ofríki	rampages, un-rule, unruly
ofstýri	unmanageable
oft	often
ok	also, and
okkars	our
okkr	us
ombun	return
orð	words
orða	words
orði	word
orðinn	become
orðit	become, words
oss	ours, us

Ó, ó

Old Norse	English
óðafári	a-hurry
óðast	furious
ófæru	impassable
ófallit	misguided
ófarin	un-faring
ófrýnligr	inconspicuous
óhæfu	unqualified
óheilagr	unholy

Word List (Old Norse to English)

Old Norse	English
ójafnaðarmenn	un-equal-men
Óláfi	Olaf (name)
Óláfr	Olaf (name)
Óláfs	Olaf's (name)
óliðdrjúgr	un-substantial-company
óliðligt	unsuitable
ólman	wild
ómæt	un-good
ómannligt	inhumane
óorðan	slanderous
ór	back-from, from, from-out-of, of, out-of
óréttvíss	un-right-knowing
Óttari	Ottar (name)
Óttarr	Ottar (name)
óvinum	un-friends
óvinveittr	unfriendly
óvíst	uncertain
óx	grew

Ö, ö

Old Norse	English
öðru	another, others
öðrum	another, other, others
öðruvís	other-knowing
öfundarmenn	slanderous-men
öll	all
öllu	all
öllum	all
öxi	axe
öxlina	an-axe

P, p

Old Norse	English
Pá	Peacock (name)

R, r

Old Norse	English
ráð	advised, decide, declare
ráða	allow, decide
ráðast	arrange
ráðlauss	ill-advised
ráðligast	advice, advisable
ráðs	advice
ræddist	discussed
ræðst	rode
réða	decide
réðst	rode
refði	poleaxe
reið	riding, rode
reifa	account-for
réttendum	right
réttvísi	right-knowing
Reykja	Reykir (place)
reyna	tested, trying
reyndi	test
ríð	ride
ríða	ride, rode, to-ride
ríðið	ride
riðinn	riding
riðit	ridden, ride
ríðr	rode
riðu	rode
rífa	tearing
Ríka	Powerful (name)
ríki	powerful
róstum	unruliness

S, s

Old Norse	English
sá	saw, so
sækir	seek
sæmð	honour
sæmðar	honour
sæmðarauki	honour
sæmðir	honour
sæmðum	honour
sæta	sit-in-ambush
sætt	settle
sættast	reconcile
safnar	collected
sagði	said, told
sagt	said, told
sakar	conviction, for-the-sake-of, for-the-sake-of, sake, the-charges
saman	the-same, together

Word List (Old Norse to English)

Old Norse	English
samit	agreement
sannast	the-truest, true, truly
sár	wound, wounding, wounds
sára	wounds
sárr	wounded
sárum	the-wounds
sat	sat, stayed
satt	TRUE
sátu	sat, sitting, stayed
sé	are, being, is, see, so, this, was
segi	say
segir	said, told
segja	say, to-say
seilast	obtain
sekðan	outlawed
sekði	convicted
selja	repay
sem	as, as-if, that, which, who
sendi	send
sér	her, him, himself, his, saw, them, themselves
setit	stay
setjast	stayed
setr	set
sett	set
settist	set
setuefni	sitting
síðan	after, afterwards, then
síðar	afterwards
síðir	eventually
Sigríðar	Sigrid (name)
Sigríði	Sigrid (name)
Sigríðr	Sigrid (name)
sik	him, himself, such
silfrs	of-silver
sín	him, his, this
sína	his, their, theirs
sinn	hers, his, theirs
sinna	his, theirs
sinni	his
síns	her, his
sínu	his
sínum	hers, his, theirs, they
sitja	sit, sit-in-ambush, sitting
sitr	stayed
sitt	his, this
sjá	saw
sjálfan	yourself
sjálfdæmi	self-judgement
sjándi	seeing
sjau	seven
skaða	scathed
Skagafirði	Skagafjord (place)
Skagafjarðar	Skagafjord (place)
skal	shall, shall-be, should
skalt	shall
skaltu	shall, shall-you
skammt	a-short-distance, short-distance
skapi	mood
skapillr	bad-temper
skaplyndi	nature
skarpasti	hardest
Skeið	Skeid (place)
Skeiði	Skeid (place)
skelmi	devilish-man
skikkju	cloak
skildi	shield
skilði	separated
skildinum	the-shield
skildir	shields
skilðist	separated
skilðu	separated
skilðust	separated
skilit	separated
skilja	separate, separated
skiljum	understanding
skilnaði	parted, parting
skinnstakki	skin-cloak
skip	a-ship
skips	ships
skipta	exchange
skipti	exchanged
skiptust	exchanged
skirra	prevent
skjöld	shield
skjöldrinn	the-shield

Word List (Old Norse to English)

Old Norse	English
skjótt	quickly
skógarmenn	forest-men
skóggang	outlawry
skóggangssök	forest-seeking
sköllóttr	bald
sköruliga	boldly
skörungr	noble
skulu	shall
skuluð	should
skulum	should
skyld	guilt
skylda	should
skyldi	should
skyldu	should
skyli	shall
skýtr	shot
sleppa	escape
slík	such
slitit	dissolved
smæri	smaller
snaghyrnda	snag-cornered
snarliga	quickly
sneri	turned
snerist	turned
snjór	snow
snúa	return, turn
sögu	saga
sögum	sagas
sóknin	the-struggle
sökótt	accusations
sömu	same
sonar	son
sonr	son, son-of, the-son-of
sótt	attend, attended, sought
sótti	sought
spara	spare
spekð	wisdom
spjót	spear
spjóti	spear
spjótinu	spear
spjótit	spear, the-spear
spretta	sprang
spyrr	asked
stað	place

Old Norse	English
staddr	standing
Stærimaðr	Stately-man (name)
Stærimann	Stately-man (name)
Stærimanni	Stately-man (name)
standanda	stood
Starri	Starri (name)
stefna	agreement
stefndi	charged, summoned
stefnir	charged
stefnu	summoned, summons
stefnuna	the-summons
stefnunni	the-summons
stela	steal, stealing
Stertimaðr	Stately-man (name)
stíga	step
stigu	dismounted
stóð	stood
stolit	stolen
stólkonungrinn	the-emperor
stórmannliga	great-man-ness
stórmannligar	great-man-like
studdist	stood
stund	while
stýrimann	the-captain
styrk	strength
suðr	south
sumar	summer
sumarit	summer
sundr	asunder
sundrþykki	discord
svá	so
svarar	answered
Svarfaðardal	Svarfadardal (place)
Svarfaðardals	Svarfadardal (place)
Svarfaðardalsár	Svarfadardal (place)
Svarfdæla	Svarfadardal (place)
svarið	answer
svartan	a-black
sveininn	the-boy
sveinsins	son-yours
sveit	company
sveitir	areas
sveitum	the-district
sverðinu	the-sword
sviptir	loss

Word List (Old Norse to English)

Old Norse	English
sýna	seemed, show
sýnir	showed
sýnist	seemed
sýnt	shown
systrungr	mother's-sister's-son

T, t

Old Norse	English
tæki	take
tækist	took
tak	take
taka	take, taken
takir	take
tal	talking
tala	said, speak, spoke
talit	conversation
tauma	reins
tekit	taken
tekizt	taken
tekr	took
tel	say
tíðenda	news
tigu	ten
til	about, its, to, until
tilfelli	occurrence
tillæti	deference
tiltekju	exchange
tíma	time
títt	reported
tók	took
tókst	took
tóku	took-to
tólf	twelve
töluðu	talked, told
torfstakka	turf-stacks
trausts	trust
Tungu	Tunga (place)
tvá	two
tvenn	twice

Þ, þ

Old Norse	English
þá	the, then, they, when
þaðan	from-there
þætti	seems
þakka	thanks
þakkaði	thanked
þakkar	thanked, thanks
þangat	from-there, there, there
þann	the, then
þar	here, it, there, there
þarf	need
þarftu	need-you
þat	is, it, so, that, this, to
þau	they
þegar	as-soon-as, from-there, immediately, then, when
þeim	home, them, they, to-them
þeir	the, then, there, they
þeira	of-them, of-they, their, theirs, them, they, they-of
þenna	this
þér	to-you, you, your
þess	this
þessa	this
þessar	these
þessi	this
þessir	these
þessu	this
þetta	that, this
þiggir	accept
þiggja	accept, accepted, to-accept
þiggr	accepted
þik	you
þína	yours
þing	assembly, the-assembly
þinginu	the-assembly
þingit	the-assembly
þingmaðr	assembly-man
þingsins	the-assembly
þinn	you, yours
þinnar	yours
þinni	yours
þit	you, you-two
þitt	yours

Word List (Old Norse to English)

Old Norse	English
þjófarnir	thieves
þjófnað	theft
þó	though
þökk	thanks
þola	endure
þora	dare
Þórð	Thord (name)
Þórðar	Thord (name)
Þórðarsonar	Son-of-Thord (name)
Þórði	Thord (name)
Þórdís	Thordis (name)
Þórðr	Thord (name)
Þorgrímr	Thorgrim (name)
Þórólf	Thorolf (name)
Þórólfi	Thorolf (name)
Þórólfr	Thorolf (name)
Þórólfs	Thorolf's (name)
Þorstein	Thorstein (name), Thorstein (name)
Þorsteini	Thorstein (name), Thorstein's (name)
Þorsteinn	Thorstein (name)
Þorsteins	Thorstein's (name)
Þorvaldi	Thorvald (name)
Þorvaldr	Thorvald (name)
þótt	though
þótti	thought
þóttu	thought
þriggja	three
þrír	three
þrjá	three
þrjár	three
þú	you
Þúfum	Thufur (place)
þungt	negatively
þurfa	need
þurfi	need
Þverá	Thvera (place)
Þverár	Thvera (place)
þvers	across
því	according, accordingly, as, because, since, such, that, therefore
þykkir	consider, seems, think, thought
þykkist	think
þykkjast	realised, think
þykkjumst	think

U, u

Old Norse	English
um	about, with
umskipti	about-exchanged
undan	away-from
undir	into, near
undri	fool-of-yourself
ungr	young
upp	up, upped
upphaf	begun
uppi	up
uppsögn	up-saying
Urðskriðuhóla	Urdskriduholar (place)
urðu	became

Ú, ú

Old Norse	English
út	from, out
útan	abroad
úti	outside

V, v

Old Norse	English
váða	risk
vænt	expect
væra	be
væri	was
værir	be, would-be
ván	expected, to-expect
vanða	custom
vandi	difficulty
vandræði	dispute
vandræðum	trouble
vápn	weapons
vápnaðir	weaponed
vápns	weapons
var	then, was, were
vár	spring
varð	became, was

Word List (Old Norse to English)

Old Norse	English
varða	warranted
várdaga	spring-days
varði	expect
varðveita	ward-knowing
varðveizlu	hospitality
varla	barely
várn	our
varna	defence
várra	ours
vartu	where
váru	was, were
veðr	weathered
veg	way
vegar	way
veit	know
veita	giving, grant
veitti	granted
veizla	feast, the-feast
veizlu	feast
vel	well
velli	the-fields
velviljaðr	well-willing
venzlum	marriage
ver	be
vér	our, we
vera	be, becomes, being, be-it, were
verð	the-worth
verða	be, became, become, being, would-be
verðgang	vagrancy
verði	become
verðr	becomes, worth
verðugt	worth
verit	been
verja	defend, guarding, protect
verk	work
versna	worse
verst	the-worst
vert	worthy
vesalmenni	wretch
vestr	west
vetra	winters
vetrinn	winter
vexti	grown

Old Norse	English
við	against, by, to, with
viðtökur	with-taken, with-taking
víg	killing, slaying-of, the-killing-of, the-slaying-of
víga	fight
vígi	the-slaying
vígsmálit	fight-the-case
vil	will, wish
vilda	wish
vildi	willing, wished
vilir	wish
vilja	will, willing, wish
viljum	will
vill	wish, wished, wishing
vin	friend
vinátta	friendship
vináttu	friendship
vindr	the-wind
vinganarmál	friendship-matter
vingast	make-friends
vinr	a-friend, friend
vinsæll	popular
vinskap	friendship
vinskapar	friendship
virða	value, worth
virðið	honour
virðing	honour, respect, worth, worthiness
virðingar	honour
virðingarvænligt	respect-kindly
virðingu	honour
virkit	the-compound
víst	certainly
vistar	lodging
vísu	certainly
vita	know
vitja	visit
vitlauss	wit-less
Völlu	Vellir (place)
Völlum	Vellir (place)

Word List (Old Norse to English)

Old Norse English

Y, y

yðr you, your
yður yours
yðvar you
yðvarn of-you
yfir over
yrði with

Word List *(English to Old Norse)*

English	Old Norse	English	Old Norse
		all-prepared	*albúnir*
A, a		all-settle	*alsáttir*
		all-well	*allvel, allvel*
a	*at*	alone	*einn*
a-black	*svartan*	along	*eftir*
a-blue	*blán*	also	*ok*
about	*á, at, en, í, til, um*	am	*em, er*
about-exchanged	*umskipti*	a-man	*maðr, mann, manni*
about-that-time	*mund*	ambush	*fyrirsát*
abroad	*útan*	a-meeting	*fundr*
a-bull	*graðung*	am-named	*heiti*
accept	*þiggir, þiggja*	a-month	*mánuð*
accepted	*þiggja, þiggr*	an	*eða*
accomplished	*fær*	an-abundance	*gnótt*
according	*því*	an-axe	*öxlina*
accordingly	*því*	and	*eða, en, er, ok*
account-for	*reifa*	anew	*nýju*
accusations	*sökótt*	an-idiot	*mannfóli*
across	*þvers*	another	*aðra, annarr, annarri, annat, öðru, öðrum*
advice	*ráðligast, ráðs*		
advisable	*ráðligast*	answer	*svarið*
advised	*ráð*	answered	*svarar*
a-farm	*bæ*	any	*einum, neins, nökkura*
a-friend	*vinr*	any-longer	*lengr*
after	*eftir, síðan*	appears	*lízt*
after-matter	*eftirmáls*	are	*er, eru, eruð, sé*
afterwards	*eftir, síðan, síðar*	areas	*sveitir*
against	*við*	are-there	*eru*
age	*aldri*	are-you	*ertu*
aggression	*ágang*	arms	*fangi*
agreed	*játtu*	Arnor (name)	*Arnóri, Arnórr*
agreement	*samit, stefna*	Arnor's (name)	*Arnórs*
a-haystack	*heyvöndul*	arrange	*ráðast*
ahead	*fyrir*	as	*á, at, er, sem, því*
a-house	*hús*	a-ship	*skip*
a-hurry	*óðafári*	a-short-distance	*skammt*
a-journey	*förum*	as-if	*sem*
a-little	*lítinn*	a-sign	*marki*
all	*alla, alla, allan, allar, allir, allir, allri, alls, allt, allt, öll, öllu, öllum*	as-in-laws	*mágsemðar*
		ask	*beiðast*
		asked	*bað, beiddi, spyrr*
all-great-man-like	*allstórmannliga*	asked-for	*heimti*
allow	*láta, ráða*	asking	*frétti*

Word List (English to Old Norse)

English	Old Norse	English	Old Norse
assembly	þing	being	sé, vera, verða
assembly-man	þingmaðr	be-it	vera
assist	greiða	belt	belti
assistance	ásjá, liðsinni, liðveizlu	benefit	beini, gott
as-soon-as	þegar	beside	hjá
asunder	sundr	best	bezt, bezta, beztr
at	á, at, í	better	bæta, betr, betra, betri
at-home	heiman	between	meðal, milli
attend	sótt	bid	boðit
attended	sótt	Bjarni (name)	Bjarnar
attention	gaumr	black	blári
away	brott	boldly	djarfliga, sköruliga
away-from	undan	Bollason (name)	Bollason, Bollasyni
awhile	hríð	Bolli (name)	Bolla, Bolli
axe	öxi	Bolli's (name)	Bolla
		both	báðir

B, b

English	Old Norse	English	Old Norse
		bound	bindr, bundinn
		bravely	drengiligsta
back	aftr, bak	break	bregða
back-from	ór	bring	færa
bad	illa	bringing	færa
bad-temper	skapillr	broke	braut, bregðr
bad-terms	illt	broke-away	hvarf
bald	sköllóttr	broken	brotit
bank	bakkann	brother	bróðir, bróður
barely	varla	brothers	bræðr
bathe	laug	buckled	gyrðr
battle	bardagi	bull	graðung, graðungr
be	væra, værir, ver, vera, verða	but	en, enn, er
bear	berr, borit	by	við
bears	barizt		

C, c

English	Old Norse	English	Old Norse
became	lagði, urðu, varð, verða		
because	því	called	heitaðist, kallaðr
because-of	fyrir	came	gengr, kemr, kom, koma, kominn, komit, kómu
become	orðinn, orðit, verða, verði		
becomes	vera, verðr	cape	kápu
bed-roll	húðfat	care	nenni
been	verit	carried	borit
before	áðr, fyrir, fyrr, fyrri	case	mál
before-us	fyrrum	cast	kasta
began	hóf	cattle	fé
begun	upphaf	celebration	fagnaði
behind	heldr	certainly	víst, vísu

58

Word List (English to Old Norse)

English	Old Norse	English	Old Norse
challenge	áskorun	decide	ráð, ráða, réða
charged	stefndi, stefnir	declare	kalla, ráð
charges	atkvæðum	deed-refuse	nauðsynja
chieftain	höfðingi	defence	varna
chieftains	höfðingjar	defend	verja
children	börnum	deference	tillæti
choosing	kýstu	describe	lýsa
chose	kostr	deserve	makligt
cloak	skikkju	devastate	eyða
close	fast, nær	devilish-man	skelmi
closely	fast	did	fór, gerði, gerðu
closely-related	náskyld	difficulty	erfit, vandi
clothing	klæði	diminish	minni
coldly	fáliga	discord	sundrþykki
collected	safnar	discourage	letja
come	kemr, kom, komim, kominn, komir, komit, komnir	discuss	máli
		discussed	ræddist
		dismounted	stigu
coming	kemr, koma, komnir	dispute	vandræði
companions	förunautar, förunautar	dissolved	slitit
company	sveit	dissuaded	letjast
company-less	liðfæri	district	fjórðungi, heðra, heraði, heruð
company-provided	liðsafla		
compensate	bæta	do	gera, gerið, gerir
compensation	fébótum	doing	gera, gerir
comrades	félagar	done	gert
comradeship	félagsskap	down	aftr, leyst, niðr, niðri, ofan
concluded	lauk		
consider	þykkir	drew	bregðr, dregr
considerable	ærin	dwelled	dvölðust
conversation	talit		
convicted	sekði		
conviction	sakar		
costume	búningr		
cowardly	íhann		
Crone's-Nose (name)	Kerlingarnef		
custom	vanða		

D, d

Dagverdarnes (place)	Dögurðarnes		
danger	hættu		
dare	þora		
dead	dauðr		
dearest	dýrsta		

E, e

English	Old Norse
each	hvárir, hvert
eager	kapp
earlier	áðr
earth	jörð
earth-house	jarðhús
easily	hægligt
eight	átta
eighteen	átján
either-side	hvárirtveggju
ells	alna
encounter	finnast
encouraged	eggjar

Word List (English to Old Norse)

English	Old Norse
endure	þola
equal	jafna
equal-many	jafnmarga
escape	sleppa
evening	kveldit
eventually	síðir
every	hverju
everyday	hversdagliga
evil	illu
exchange	skipta, tiltekju
exchanged	skipti, skiptust
expect	ætla, vænt, varði
expected	ván

F, f

English	Old Norse
failed	fallit
fair	fögrum
fairly	haga
fallen	fallit, fallnir
falling	felldr
false	
falsehood	fólsku
famous-work	frægðarverk
far-away	fjarri
fared	farit
farm	bæ, búi
farmer	bóndi
farmhouse	bænum
fast	fast
fastened	fast
feast	veizla, veizlu
fee	fá, fé
fell	fellr
few	fáir, fár, fátt
fiendship	fjandskap
fifteen	fimmtán
fight	berist, berjast, víga
fight-the-case	vígsmálit
find	finna, finnim, hitt
finished	lokit
floating	flaut
flock	flokk
follow	fylgja
followed	flýgr, fylgir, fylgt
followers-many	fjölmenni
following-men	fjölmenna
follows	fylg, fylgi
foolish	afglapa
foolishly	fólit, heimskliga, heimskligast
foolishness	heimskr
fool-of-yourself	undri
for	á, at, fyrir, í
forest-men	skógarmenn
forest-seeking	skóggangssök
for-me	mér
for-the-ambush	fyrirsátina
for-the-sake-of	sakar, sakar
fortunate	hamingja
fought	berjast
found	fann, fekk, fundust
frenzy-man	æðimaðr
friend	vin, vinr
friendship	kærleik, vinátta, vináttu, vinskap, vinskapar
friendship-matter	vinganarmál
from	á, af, af, at, frá, fram, ór, út
from-here	heðan
from-home	heiman
from-home-travel	heimanferð
from-out-of	ór
from-there	þaðan, þangat, þegar
full-of-people	fjölmennt
furious	óðast

G, g

English	Old Norse
Galmarstrond (place)	Galmarströnd
game	leik
gave	gaf, gáfu
gets	fengi
gifts	gjafar, gjöfum
give	gefa, gefið
given	gefinn
giving	veita
gladdest	glaðasti
go	fara, ganga
goes	ferr, fór

Word List (English to Old Norse)

English	Old Norse	English	Old Norse
going	fara, ferðina, ferr, gangi	have	at, áttir, eiga, ert, haf, hafa, hafast, hafið, hafir, haft, hefi, hefir, höfum, leggja
gold-inlaid	gullrekna		
gold-laid	gulllagðan		
gold-ring	fingrgull, gullhring, gullhringinn, gullhringr	have-right	heimul
		have-you	áttu
gone	farin, farit, gengit	hay	hey, heyjum
good	góða, góðar, góðr, góðum	hay-bundle	heyvöndul
		hay-giving	heygjöfinni
got	fá, fær, fekk, getit, getr	haystacks	andvirki
grab	grípa	hay-stacks	heygarð
grant	veita	he	hana, hann, honum
granted	veitti	head	höfuð
great	mikill, mikinn, miklir, mjök	healed	greru
		heard	heyrði, heyrir, heyrt
greatly	ágætliga, harðla	Hegranes (place)-Assembly	Hegranessþingi, Hegranessþings
great-man-like	stórmannligar		
great-man-ness	stórmannliga	held	helt
greeted	kvaddi	Helgi (name)	Helga, Helgi
greeting	kveddi	Helgi's (name)	Helga
grew	óx	Heljardal Heath (place)	Heljardalsheiði
grey	grán	Hellu-Narfason (name)	Hellu-Narfasonar
grown	vexti	Hellu-Narfi (name)	Hellu-Narfa
guarding	verja	helmet	hjálm
Guddalir (place)	Guðdölum	her	hana, henni, sér, síns
Gudmund (name)	Guðmundar, Guðmundr	herd	hrossin
Gudrun (name)	Guðrún	here	hér, hingat, þar
guilt	skyld	hers	hennar, sinn, sínum
		Hestanes (place)	Hestanesi
		hey	hey
# H, h		him	hann, hans, honum, sér, sik, sín
had	átt, átti, áttu, er, hafa, hafði, hafi, haft, hefir, hefr, höfðu, lætr, lagt, lét	himself	sér, sik
		his	hann, hans, honum, sér, sín, sína, sinn, sinna, sinni, síns, sínu, sínum, sitt
half	hálfan, hválfinu		
half-month's	hálfsmánaðar		
Hals (place)	Háls, Hálsi	his-hands	höndum
hand	hendi, hendr, hönd, höndum	Hjaltadal (place)	Hjaltadal
		Hjaltasons (name)	Hjaltasona, Hjaltasonu, Hjaltasynir
hardest	harðasta, skarpasti		
harm	mein	Hjardarholt (place)	Hjarðarholti
has	at, hafði, hefði, hefir, höfum	Hof (place)	Hofi, Hofs
		Hofdi (place)	Höfða
		hold	halda
		holds	haldinn
		hollow	holinu

Word List (English to Old Norse)

English	Old Norse	English	Old Norse
home	heim, heima, þeim	intend	ætla, ætlar
home-invitation	heimboðanna	intended	ætla, ætlar, ætlat
home-invitations	heimboðum	into	á, í, undir
homes	alizt	invited	bauð, býðr
home-sought	heimsótt	iron-shod	járna
home-ways	heimleiðis	is	er, eru, í, sé, þat
honour	drengskap, frama, frama, framar, sæmð, sæmðar, sæmðarauki, sæmðir, sæmðum, virðið, virðing, virðingar, virðingu	it	á, at, í, þar, þat
		it-is	er
		its	til
hooves	klaufir		
horn	horn	## J, j	
horse	hest, hesti		
horseback	baki	journey	ferð, ferðir, leið
horses	fararskjóta, hesta, hestana	joyfulness	blíðu
horse's	hestsins	## K, k	
hospitality	varðveizlu		
host	bóndi	kill	drepa, drepit
housewife	húsfreyja, húsfreyju	killing	drepit, víg
how	hvárt, hversu, hvert	king's-gift	konungsnaut
how-so	hversu	kinsman	frænda, niðr
Hrutafjord (place)	Hrútafirði, Hrútafjarðar	kinswoman	frændkona, frændkonu
hundred	hundruð	knife	kníf
hung	hekk	know	kunna, veit, vita
husband	bónda	Krossar (place)	Krossa, Krossum

I, i

L, l

English	Old Norse	English	Old Norse
I	ek, mér	laid	lagðr
ice	íss	land	löndum
if	ef	laughed	brosti
ill	ill, illa, illt	law	lögum
ill-advised	ráðlauss	law-man	málamaðr
ill-words	illyrði	lay	leggið, leggja, liggr
immediately	þegar	leapt	hljóp
impassable	ófæru	learned	frétti
in	á, at, eiga, en, í	leave	láta
inconspicuous	ófrýnligr	led	létu
inhumane	ómannligt	Leg-Biter (name)	Fótbít
in-laws	mágsemð	less	laus, minni
in-sharing-together	íhlutunarsamr	let	látum, lét, léti, létu
inside	inn, innan	little	lítill, lítils, lítit, litlu
		lived	bjó, bjuggu

Word List (English to Old Norse)

English	Old Norse	English	Old Norse
Ljot (name)	*Ljóti, Ljótr*	Miklabaer (place)	*Miklabæ*
Ljot (place)	*Ljóti, Ljóts*	mine	*mér, mik, mín, mína, minn, minna, mínum, mitt*
Ljot's (name)	*Ljóts*		
loath	*leiða*		
lodging	*vistar*	misguided	*ófallit*
long	*lengi*	mockery	*hæðilig*
longer	*lengri*	Modruvellir (place)	*Möðruvöllu*
look	*leita, líta*	mood	*skapi*
looked	*litu*	more	*fleiri, meir, meira*
looks	*horfist*	morning	*morgininn*
loss	*sviptir*	most	*mest, mesta, mestum*
lot	*hlut*	mother's-sister's-son	*systrungr*
lowly-deed	*níðingsverk*	mourned	*harmaði*
luck	*hamingja, heill*	much	*margt, mik, mikill, mikilli, mikinn, mikit, mikla, miklu, miklum, mjök*
luck-promised	*giftuvænligr*		
lunged	*lagði, leggr*		
		my	*mik, mín, mína, mínum*

M, m

N, n

English	Old Norse	English	Old Norse
made	*ger, gerð, gerði, gerðu, gert*	name	*nafn, nafn*
make	*fallit, gerðinni*	named	*heitinn, heitir, hét*
make-friends	*vingast*	Narfason (name)	*Narfason*
man	*maðr, manni*	nature	*skaplyndi*
man-of-law	*málamaðr*	near	*nær, undir*
many	*marga, margt, mjök, mörgu*	nearest	*næst*
		near-to	*náliga*
many-men	*fjölmenna*	necessity	*nauðsyn*
Marbaeli (place)	*Marbæli, Marbælinga*	need	*þarf, þurfa, þurfi*
marks	*merkr*	need-you	*þarftu*
marriage	*venzlum*	negatively	*þungt*
married	*átti, gjaforð*	neither	*hvergi*
matter	*efni, mál, máli*	never	*aldri*
may	*má, mætti, máttu, mega, megi, megum*	new	*nýjum*
		news	*frétt, tíðenda*
me	*mér, mik*	nights	*nætr*
meet	*fund, mæta, metast, móti, móts*	no	*eigi, ekki, engi, engrar*
		noble	*skörungr*
meeting	*mót*	noblest	*göfgustu*
men	*mann, manna, menn, mönnum*	none	*eigi, enga, engi, engir, engis, engrar*
merriest	*kátasti*	nor	*ne*
met	*finnast, fundust, hitti, hittir, hittust*	north	*norðan, norðr*
		northerners	*norðlendingum*
middle	*miðjan*	not	*eigi, ekki*
might	*mætta*		

63

Word List (English to Old Norse)

English	Old Norse	English	Old Norse
nothing	ekki, engu		
now	nú		

O, o

P, p

English	Old Norse	English	Old Norse
obtain	ná, seilast	parted	skilnaði
occurrence	tilfelli	parting	skilnaði
of	á, af, af, at, ór	passed	leið, líðr
of-all	allra	pay	aura, gjalda
off	af	peace	kyrrt
of-family-small	ættsmár	peaceful	fríð
offer	beiða, biðja, bjóða	Peacock (name)	Pá
offered	boðit	people	menn, mönnum
of-silver	silfrs	people's	manna
often	oft	person	manninn
of-them	þeira	place	stað
of-they	þeira	plans	ætlat
of-violent-language	málóði	pledged	hét
of-wealth	fjár	plenty-of	ærit
of-you	yðvarn	plotting	fjörráð
Olaf (name)	Óláfi, Óláfr	plotting-against	fjörráð
Olaf's (name)	Óláfs	poleaxe	refði
on	á, í	poorly	fáliga
one	eina, einhvern, einn	popular	vinsæll
one-agreement	einsætt	possible	hægt
only	einir, einn	postpone	fresta
open-whole	hliðhollir	powerful	ríki
opposite	hvárir	Powerful (name)	Ríka
or	eða	prepare	búast
ordered	bað	prepared	bjóst, búin, búit, býr, býst
other	annat, öðrum	preparing	búnir
other-knowing	öðruvís	prevent	skirra
others	aðrir, öðru, öðrum	pride	metnaðr
Ottar (name)	Óttari, Óttarr	promised	hét
our	okkars, várn, vér	promising	efniligastr
ours	oss, várra	protect	verja
out	út	provinces	heruðum
outlawed	sekðan		
outlawry	skóggang		

Q, q

English	Old Norse
out-of	ór
outside	úti
over	yfir
overcome	barst
own	eign, eigna

quickly	skjótt, snarliga

R, r

rampages	ofríki

Word List (English to Old Norse)

English	Old Norse	English	Old Norse
ran	hleypa, hleypr, hljóp, hljópu	say	segi, segja, tel
rather	heldr, helzt	scathed	skaða
realised	þykkjast	see	sé
recoiled	hrökkva	seeing	sjándi
reconcile	sættast	seek	leita, leitast, sækir
rectify	leiðréttu	seemed	sýna, sýnist
refuse	níta	seems	þætti, þykkir
reins	tauma	self-judgement	dóm, sjálfdæmi
releasing	leystr	send	sendi
relieved	fegin, létti, léttu	separate	skilja
renowned	ágætir	separated	skilði, skilðist, skilðu, skilðust, skilit, skilja
repay	selja	serves	gegnir
reported	fréttist, fréttust, títt	set	setr, sett, settist
resolved	greiddist	set-out	ferr
respect	virðing	settle	sætt
respect-kindly	virðingarvænligt	settlers	búa
rest	æja	seven	sjau
return	aftr, móti, ombun, snúa	several	nökkura
returned	aftr	shall	mun, munu, munuð, munum, skal, skalt, skaltu, skulu, skyli
Reykir (place)	Reykja		
rich	auðigr		
ridden	riðit	shall-be	skal
ride	ríð, ríða, ríðið, riðit	shall-you	muntu, skaltu
riding	reið, riðinn	she	hon
right	réttendum	shield	skildi, skjöld
right-knowing	réttvísi	shields	skildir
risk	váða	shining	blika
river	ána	ships	skips
rocks	grjóti	short-distance	skammt
rode	ræðst, réðst, reið, ríða, ríðr, riðu	shot	skýtr
		should	mun, muna, muni, munt, munu, munum, mynda, myndi, skal, skuluð, skulum, skylda, skyldi, skyldu
running	hlaupi		

S, s

		should-you	muntu
		show	lýsa, sýna
safe	fritt, heilir	showed	sýnir
saga	sögu	shown	lýst, sýnt
sagas	sögum	side	hlið
said	kvað, lézt, sagði, sagt, segir, tala	sides	megin
		Sigrid (name)	Sigríðar, Sigríði, Sigríðr
sake	sakar	since	en, því
same	sömu	sit	sitja
sat	sat, sátu	sit-in-ambush	sæta, sitja
saw	leit, sá, sér, sjá		

Word List (English to Old Norse)

English	Old Norse	English	Old Norse
sitting	sátu, setuefni, sitja	stealing	stela
Skagafjord (place)	Skagafirði, Skagafjarðar	step	stíga
Skeid (place)	Skeið, Skeiði	still	kyrrt
skin-cloak	skinnstakki	stolen	stolit
slander	illmæli	stood	standanda, stóð, studdist
slanderous	óorðan		
slanderous-men	öfundarmenn	stop	hættu
slaying-of	víg	strength	styrk
smaller	smæri	striking	höggr
snag-cornered	snaghyrnda	such	sik, slík, því
snow	snjór	summer	sumar, sumarit
so	sá, sé, svá, þat	summoned	stefndi, stefnu
solved	leyst	summons	stefnu
some	nökkurir, nökkut	suspect	grunr
something	nökkut	suspected	grunaði
somewhat	nökkura, nökkurr, nökkut	Svarfadardal (place)	Svarfaðardal, Svarfaðardals, Svarfaðardalsár, Svarfdæla
son	sonar, sonr		
son-of	sonr		
Son-of-Bolli (name)	Bollason		
Son-of-Thord (name)	Þórðarsonar		
Sons-of-Hjalti (name)	Hjaltasynir		

T, t

English	Old Norse
son-yours	sveinsins
sought	sótt, sótti
south	suðr
spare	spara
speak	máli, tala
speaking	mælti
speak-to	mál
spear	spjót, spjóti, spjótinu, spjótit
spoke	kvað, mælti, mæltu, tala
sport	leika, leikim
sprang	spretta
spring	vár
spring-days	várdaga
spurred	keyrði, keyrir
standing	staddr
Starri (name)	Starri
Starri-of-Guddalir	guðdala-starra
startled	brá
Stately-man (name)	Stærimaðr, Stærimann, Stærimanni, Stertimaðr
stay	setit
stayed	sat, sátu, setjast, sitr
steal	stela

English	Old Norse
take	tæki, tak, taka, takir
taken	taka, tekit, tekizt
talked	mælt, töluðu
talking	tal
team-minded	liðsinnaðr
tearing	rífa
ten	tigu
test	freista, reyndi
tested	reyna
than	en
thanked	kvað, þakkaði, þakkar
thanks	þakka, þakkar, þökk
that	at, en, er, í, sem, þat, þetta, því
the	á, at, enn, er, hinu, í, in, ina, inn, ins, inum, it, þá, þann, þeir
the-after-matter	eftirmálinu
the-assembly	alþingi, þing, þinginu, þingit, þingsins
the-battle	bardagann
the-booth	búðina
the-booth-doors	búðardurunum
the-boy	sveininn

Word List (English to Old Norse)

English	*Old Norse*	English	*Old Norse*
the-brothers	*bræðra*	the-shield	*skildinum, skjöldrinn*
the-bull	*boli, graðungrinn*	the-slaying	*vígi*
the-captain	*stýrimann*	the-slaying-of	*víg*
the-case	*málinu, málit*	the-slope	*hlíðinni*
the-charges	*sakar*	the-son-of	*sonr*
the-compound	*virkit*	the-spear	*spjótit*
the-district	*sveitum*	the-struggle	*sóknin*
the-earth	*jörð*	the-summons	*stefnuna, stefnunni*
the-emperor	*stólkonungrinn*	the-sword	*sverðinu*
the-farm	*bæinn, bænum, bú*	the-truest	*sannast*
the-farmer	*bónda, bóndi*	the-unseen-man	*launmaðrinn*
the-feast	*veizla*	the-way	*leiðina*
the-fields	*velli*	the-wind	*vindr*
theft	*þjófnað*	the-worst	*verst*
the-gift	*gjafar*	the-worth	*verð*
the-gifts	*gjafarnar*	the-wounds	*sárum*
the-hay	*desjarnar, heyinu*	they	*sínum, þá, þau, þeim, þeir, þeira*
the-heath	*heiðina*		
the-horses	*hestana*	they-of	*þeira*
the-ice	*ísinn*	thieves	*þjófarnir*
their	*sína, þeira*	things	*hlutir*
theirs	*sína, sinn, sinna, sínum, þeira*	think	*hugða, hugðum, hygg, hyggja, þykkir, þykkist, þykkjast, þykkjumst*
the-journey	*ferðinni*		
the-killing-of	*víg*	this	*í, sé, sín, sitt, þat, þenna, þess, þessa, þessi, þessu, þetta*
the-leg	*fæti*		
them	*sér, þeim, þeira*		
the-man	*maðrinn, mannsins*	Thord (name)	*Þórð, Þórðar, Þórði, Þórðr*
the-matter	*efni, mál, máli, málit, málum*		
		Thordis (name)	*Þórdís*
the-middle	*miðri*	Thorgrim (name)	*Þorgrímr*
the-more	*meiri*	Thorolf (name)	*Þórólf, Þórólfi, Þórólfr*
themselves	*sér*	Thorolf's (name)	*Þórólfs*
then	*en, enn, er, síðan, þá, þann, þegar, þeir, var*	Thorstein (name)	*Þorstein, Þorstein, Þorsteini, Þorsteinn*
the-night	*nóttina*	Thorstein's (name)	*Þorsteini, Þorsteins*
the-northerners	*norðlendinga*	Thorvald (name)	*Þorvaldi, Þorvaldr*
the-pastures	*afréttum*	though	*þó, þótt*
there	*eru, þangat, þangat, þar, þar, þeir*	thought	*hugðu, hugsar, þótti, þóttu, þykkir*
therefore	*því*	threat	*hót*
the-ring	*hringinn*	three	*þriggja, þrír, þrjá, þrjár*
the-river	*áin, ána, ána, ánni, ár, árinnar*	through	*gegnum*
		Thufur (place)	*Þúfum*
the-same	*saman*	Thvera (place)	*Þverá, Þverár*
these	*ina, þessar, þessir*	time	*tíma*

Word List (English to Old Norse)

English	Old Norse	English	Old Norse
to	á, áðu, af, at, átzt, í, þat, til, við	turned	hallaði, sneri, snerist
to-accept	þiggja	twelve	tólf
to-do	gera	twice	tvenn
to-expect	ván	two	tvá
together	jafnsaman, saman		
to-give	gefa		
to-going	atgöngu		

U, u

English	Old Norse
to-have	eiga, hafa
to-him	honum
to-invite	bjóða
told	sagði, sagt, segir, töluðu
to-me	mér
took	tækist, tekr, tók, tókst
took-to	tóku
to-people	mönnum
to-ride	ríða
to-say	segja
to-them	þeim
to-travel	fara
to-you	þér
trading-men	kaupmenn, kaupmönnum
travel	færi, fara, farið, ferð, ferðar, ferðinni, ferr
travelled	fær, farit, ferr, fór, fóru
travelled-you	fórtu
travelling	farinn, ferð
travels	ferr
treacherous	fláráðum
treachery	brekráð
treasures	gripirnir
trim	kvista
trouble	vandræðum
true	
true	
truly	sannast
trust	trausts
try	freista
trying	reyna
Tunga (place)	Tungu
tunic	kyrtil
turf-stacks	torfstakka
turn	horfa, hverfa, hverfið, snúa

English	Old Norse
unanimously	einhlítt
uncertain	óvíst
understanding	skiljum
un-equal-men	ójafnaðarmenn
un-faring	ófarin
unfriendly	óvinveittr
un-friends	óvinum
un-good	ómæt
unholy	óheilagr
unmanageable	ofstýri
unqualified	óhæfu
un-right-knowing	óréttvíss
un-rule	ofríki
unruliness	róstum
unruly	ofríki
un-substantial-company	óliðdrjúgr
unsuitable	óliðligt
until	til
up	á, upp, uppi
upped	upp
up-saying	uppsögn
Urdskriduholar (place)	Urðskriðuhóla
us	okkr, oss
usually	jafnan

V, v

English	Old Norse
vagrancy	verðgang
value	virða
Vellir (place)	Völlu, Völlum
visit	vitja

W, w

English	Old Norse
wait	bíðr
ward-knowing	varðveita

Word List (English to Old Norse)

English	Old Norse	English	Old Norse
warranted	varða	words	orð, orða, orðit
warriors	kappi	work	verk
was	á, en, er, sé, væri, var, varð, váru	worse	versna
		worth	verðr, verðugt, virða, virðing
was-named	hét	worthiness	virðing
way	leið, veg, vegar	worthy	göfugt, vert
way-out	færi	would	mun, mundu, muni, munu, myndi
we	vér		
wealth	fé, fjár	would-be	munu, værir, verða
weaponed	vápnaðir	wound	sár
weapons	vápn, vápns	wounded	meiddi, sárr
weathered	veðr	wounding	sár
we-get	hljótum	wounds	sár, sára
welcomed	fagnat	wretch	vesalmenni
well	fellu, vel		
well-willing	velviljaðr		
went	fór, fóru, ganga, gekk, gengr, gengu		

Y, y

English	Old Norse
were	er, eru, var, váru, vera
west	vestr
what	en, hvar, hvat, hverja, hvern, hvert
when	er, nær, þá, þegar
where	hvar, vartu
whether	en, hvárt
which	er, hvert, sem
while	stund
white	hvítr
who	er, hverir, hverr, sem
wife	kona, konu
wife-of	kona
wild	ólman
will	vil, vilja, viljum
willing	vildi, vilja
winter	vetrinn
winters	vetra
wisdom	spekð
wish	vil, vilda, vilir, vilja, vill
wished	vildi, vill
wishing	vill
with	á, með, um, við, yrði
with-fleetness	flytir
with-taken	viðtökur
with-taking	viðtökur
wit-less	vitlauss
word	orði

English	Old Norse
you	þér, þik, þinn, þit, þú, yðr, yðvar
young	ungr
your	þér, yðr
yours	þína, þinn, þinnar, þinni, þitt, yður
yourself	sjálfan
you-two	þit
Yule (name)	Jól

The Tale of Bolli Bollason (Old Icelandic)

The Tale of Bolli Bollason (*Old Icelandic*)

Old Icelandic	Literal	English
1	1	1
Í þann tíma er Bolli Bollason bjó í Tungu og nú var áður frá sagt þá bjó norður í Skagafirði á Miklabæ Arnór kerlingarnef son Bjarnar Þórðarsonar frá Höfða.	At the time that Bolli Bollason lived at Tunga also now was earlier from told then lived north in Skagafjord in Miklabaer Arnor Crone's-Nose son-of Bjarni Son-of-Thord from Hofdi.	At the same time that Bolli Bollason lived at Tunga, as was spoken of earlier, Arnor Crone's-Nose lived north at Skagafjord in Miklabaer, he was the son of Bjarni Thordarson from Hofdi.
Þórður hét maður er bjó á Marbæli.	Thord named a-man who lived at Marbaeli.	There was a man named Thord who lived at Marbaeli.
Guðrún hét kona hans.	Gudrun named wife his.	His wife was named Gudrun.
Þau voru vel að sér og höfðu gnótt fjár.	They were well of themselves and had an-abundance of-wealth.	They were fine people and had an abundance of wealth.
Son þeirra hét Ólafur og var hann ungur að aldri og allra manna efnilegastur.	Son theirs named Olaf and was he young in age and of-all men promising.	Their son was named Olaf, and he was young and the most promising of all men.
Guðrún kona Þórðar var náskyld Bolla Bollasyni.	Gudrun wife-of Thord was closely-related Bolli Bollason.	Gudrun, Thord's wife, was closely related to Bolli Bollason.
Var hún systrungur hans.	Was she mother's-sister's-son his.	She was his cousin.
Ólafur son þeirra Þórðar var heitinn eftir Ólafi pá í Hjarðarholti.	Olaf son theirs Thord was named after Olaf Peacock in Hjardarholt.	Their son Olaf was named after Olaf Peacock in Hjardarholt.
Þórður og Þorvaldur Hjaltasynir bjuggu að Hofi í Hjaltadal.	Thord and Thorvald Sons-of-Hjalti lived at Hof in Hjaltadal.	Thord and Thorvald Hjaltason lived at Hof in Hjaltadal.
Þeir voru höfðingjar miklir.	They were chieftains great.	They were great chieftains.
Maður hét Þórólfur og var kallaður stertimaður.	A-man was-named Thorolf and was called Stately-man.	There was a man named Thorolf and he was called Stuck-up.
Hann bjó í Þúfum.	He lived in Thufur.	He lived at Thufur.

The Tale of Bolli Bollason (Old Icelandic)

Old Icelandic	Literal	English
Hann var óvinveittur í skapi og æðimaður mikill.	He was unfriendly in mood and frenzy-man much.	He was unfriendly in nature and a very angry man.
Hann átti griðung grán, ólman.	He had a-bull grey, wild.	He had a wild grey bull.
Þórður af Marbæli var í förum með Arnóri.	Thord of Marbaeli was on a-journey with Arnor.	Thord of Marbaeli was travelling with Arnor.
Þórólfur stærimaður átti frændkonu Arnórs en hann var þingmaður Hjaltasona.	Thorolf Stately-man married kinswoman Arnor's and he was assembly-man Hjaltasons.	Thorolf Stuck-up married one of Arnor's kinswomen, and was one of the assembly men of the Hjaltasons.
Hann átti illt við búa sína og lagði það í vanda sinn.	He had bad-terms with settlers his and became that in custom his.	He was on bad terms with his neighbours and that became the custom.
Kom það mest til þeirra Marbælinga.	Came that most to they-of Marbaeli.	And most of this came to the people of Marbaeli.
Graðungur hans gerði mönnum margt mein þá er hann kom úr afréttum.	Bull his made people many harm then as he came back-from the-pastures.	His bull did many people harm, when he came back from the pastures.
Meiddi hann fé manna en gekk eigi undan grjóti.	Wounded he cattle people's and went not away-from rocks.	He wounded people's cattle, and could not be made to go away with rocks.
Hann braut og andvirki og gerði margt illt.	He broke also haystacks and did much ill.	He also damaged haystacks and did much harm.
Þórður af Marbæli hitti Þórólf að máli og bað hann varðveita graðung sinn:	Thord of Marbaeli met Thorolf to discuss and asked him ward-knowing bull his.	Thord of Marbaeli met Thorolf to discuss this with him, and asked him to watch guard over his bull.
"Viljum vér eigi þola honum ofríki".	"Will we not endure his rampages".	"Will we not endure his rampages".
Þórólfur lést eigi mundu sitja að fé sínu.	Thorolf said not would sit at cattle his.	Thorold said that he would not sit by his cattle.
Fer Þórður heim við svo búið.	Travelled Thord home with so prepared.	Thord travelled home with this reply.
Eigi miklu síðar getur Þórður að líta hvar graðungurinn hefir brotið niður torfstakka hans.	Not much afterwards got Thord that look where the-bull had broken down turf-stacks his.	Not long afterwards Thord noticed that the bull had torn apart his stacks of turf.

The Tale of Bolli Bollason (Old Icelandic)

Old Icelandic	Literal	English
Þórður hleypur þá til og hefir spjót í hendi og er boli sér það veður hann jörð svo að upp tekur um klaufir.	Thord ran then to and had spear in hand and when the-bull saw that weathered he earth so that up took about hooves.	Thord then ran over with a spear in his hand, and when he saw it, the bull beat the ground and took up on his hooves.
Þórður leggur til hans svo að hann fellur dauður á jörð.	Thord lunged to him so that he fell dead to the-earth.	Thord lunged at him so that he fell dead on the ground.
Þórður hitti Þórólf og sagði honum að boli var dauður.	Thord met Thorolf and told him that the-bull was dead.	Thord met Thorolf and told him, that the-bull was dead.
"Þetta var lítið frægðarverk", svarar Þórólfur, "en gera mundi eg það vilja er þér þætti eigi betur".	"This was little famous-work", answered Thorolf, "and do should I that will that to-you seems not better".	"This deed is of little honour", answered Thorolf, "and I should wish to do to you something that is no better".
Þórólfur var málóði og heitaðist í hverju orði.	Thorolf was of-violent-language and called at every word.	Thorolf called on violent language with every word.
Þórður átti heimanferð fyrir höndum.	Thord had from-home-travel before his-hands.	Thord had to leave his farm.
Ólafur sonur hans var þá sjö vetra eða átta.	Olaf son his was then seven winters or eight.	His son Olaf was then seven or eight winters.
Hann fór af bænum með leik sínum og gerði sér hús sem börnum er títt en Þórólfur kom þar að honum.	He went off the-farm with game his and made himself a-house which children are reported then Thorolf came there at him.	He went away from the farm and played a game of making himself a house, which children often do, and then Thorolf came at him.
Hann lagði sveininn í gegnum með spjóti.	He lunged the-boy in through with spear.	He lunged through the boy with a spear.
Síðan fór hann heim og sagði konu sinni.	Afterwards travelled he home and told wife his.	Afterwards he travelled home and told his wife.
Hún svarar:	She answered.	She answered:
"Þetta er illt verk og ómannlegt.	"This is ill work and inhumane.	"This is an evil and inhumane deed.
Mun þér þetta illu reifa".	Shall you this evil account-for".	You shall account for this evil".
En er hún tók á honum þungt þá fór hann í brott þaðan og létti eigi fyrr en hann kom á Miklabæ til Arnórs.	Since that she took of him negatively then travelled he to away from-there and relieved not before that he came to Miklabaer to Arnor's.	Since she responded so negatively, he then travelled away and did not rest until he came to Miklabaer to Arnor.

The Tale of Bolli Bollason (Old Icelandic)

Old Icelandic	Literal	English
Fréttust þeir tíðinda.	Reported they news.	They exchanged news.
Þórólfur segir honum víg Ólafs:	Thorolf told him slaying-of Olaf's.	Thorolf told him of the killing of Olaf.
"Sé eg þar nú til trausts sem þér eruð sakir mágsemdar".	"See I here now to trust that you are sake as-in-laws".	"I look here to trust in you, for my sake, as we are in-laws".
"Eigi ferð þú sjáandi eftir um þenna hlut", sagði Arnór, "að eg muni virða meira mágsemd við þig en virðing mína og sæmd, og ásjá áttu hér engrar von af mér".	"Not going you seeing after about this lot", said Arnor, "that I should worth more in-laws with you than worth my and honour, and assistance have-you here none to-expect of me".	"You will not see it after this", said Arnor, "as I do not value my in-laws more than my honour, and you have no assistance to expect from me".
Fór Þórólfur upp eftir Hjaltadal til Hofs og fann þá Hjaltasonu og sagði þeim hvar komið var hans máli "og sé eg hér nú til ásjá sem þið eruð".	Travelled Thorolf up after Hjaltadal to Hof and found then Hjaltasons and told them what came was his matter "and being I here now to assistance as you-two are".	Thorolf travelled for Hof in Hjaltadal and found the Hjaltasons and told them what had happened, "and I am here now to ask for your assistance, as you are".
Þórður svarar:	Thord answered.	Thord answered:
"Slíkt eru níðingsverk og mun eg enga ásjá veita þér um þetta efni".	"Such is lowly-deed and should I none assistance grant to-you about this matter".	"This is such a lowly deed, and I should grant you no assistance in this matter".
Þorvaldur varð um fár.	Thorvald was about few.	Thorvald was of few words.
Fær Þórólfur ekki af þeim að sinni.	Got Thorolf nothing from them in his.	Thorolf got nothing from them in this matter.
Reið hann í brott og upp eftir Hjaltadal til Reykja, fór þar í laug.	Rode he to away and up after Hjaltadal to Reykir, went there to bathe.	He rode away for Hjaltadal to Reykir, where he went to bathe.
En um kveldið reið hann ofan aftur og undir virkið að Hofi og ræddist við einn saman svo sem annar maður væri fyrir og kveddi hann og frétti hver þar væri kominn.	Then about evening rode he down back and near the-compound at Hof and discussed with alone together so as another man were before and greeting him and asking who there was come.	Then in the evening he rode back down near the farmhouse at Hof where he spoke to himself, as if someone was standing there, who greeted him and asked who was there.
"Eg heiti Þórólfur", kvað hann.	"I am-named Thorolf", said he.	"I am named Thorolf", he said.

The Tale of Bolli Bollason (Old Icelandic)

Old Icelandic	Literal	English
"Hvert varstu farinn eða hvað er þér á höndum?" spyr launmaðurinn.	"Which where travelling and what is your in hand?" asked the-unseen-man.	"Where are you travelling, and what is your problem?" asked the unseen man.
Þórólfur segir tilfelli þessi öll eftir því sem voru:	Thorolf told occurrence this all after accordingly as was.	Thorolf told him all that had occurred.
"Bað eg Hjaltasonu ásjár", segir hann, "sakir nauðsynja minna".	"Asked I Hjaltasons assistance", said he, "for-the-sake-of deed-refuse mine".	"I asked for the Hjaltasons assistance", he said, "for the sake of my assistance".
Þessi svarar er fyrir skyldi vera:	This answered who before should be.	The man who should be before him answered:
"Gengið er nú þaðan er þeir gerðu erfið það hið fjölmenna er tólf hundruð manna sátu að og ganga slíkir höfðingjar mjög saman er nú vilja eigi veita einum manni nokkura ásjá".	"Gone are now from-there that they made difficulty that the many-men were twelve hundred men sitting about and went such chieftains many together are now willing not grant any man any assistance".	"They are now gone, they who made the difficulty with many men, there were twelve hundred sitting about, and many such chieftains went together, who are not willing to grant any man assistance".
Þorvaldur var úti staddur og heyrði talið.	Thorvald was outside standing and heard conversation.	Thorvald was standing outside and heard the conversation.
Hann gengur þangað til og tók í tauma hestsins og bað hann af baki stíga "en þó er eigi virðingarvænlegt við þig að eiga fyrir sakir fólsku þinnar".	He went there to and took the reins horse's and asked him off horseback step "but though is not respect-kindly with you to have before conviction false yours".	He went over and took the reins of the horse and asked him to step off horseback, "but it is not with honour to help a man before me with a conviction as false as yours".

2

Nú er að segja frá Þórði er hann kom heim og frá víg sonar síns og harmaði það mjög.	Now is to say from Thord that he came home and from the-slaying-of son his and mourned that much.	Now the story turns to Thord, who came home and learned of the killing of his sun, and mourned it very much.
Guðrún kona hans mælti:	Gudrun wife his spoke.	His wife Gudrun spoke:
"Það er þér ráð að lýsa vígi sveinsins á hönd Þórólfi en eg mun ríða suður til Tungu og finna Bolla frænda minn og vita hvern styrk hann vill veita okkur til eftirmáls".	"It is to-you declare that describe the-slaying son-yours in hand Thorolf and I should ride south to Tunga and find Bolli kinsman mine and know what strength he wished grant us to after-matter".	"It is for you to declare Thorolf responsible for the slaying of your son, and I shall ride south to Tunga and find Bolli my kinsman, and know what help he is willing to grant us to gain redress".

The Tale of Bolli Bollason (Old Icelandic)

Old Icelandic	Literal	English
Þau gerðu svo.	They did so.	This they did.
Og er Guðrún kom í Tungu fær hún þar viðtökur góðar.	And was Gudrun come to Tunga travelled she there with-taking good.	And when Gudrun came to Tunga, she was given a good welcome.
Hún segir Bolla víg Ólafs sonar síns og beiddi að hann tæki við eftirmálinu.	She said Bolli killing Olaf's son her and asked that he take with the-after-matter.	She told Bolli about the killing of her son Olaf, and asked that he take over the prosecution of the case.
Hann svarar:	He answered.	He answered:
"Eigi þykir mér þetta svo hæglegt að seilast til sæmdar í hendur þeim Norðlendingum.	"Not seems to-me this so easily to obtain to honour in hand they Northerners.	"It does not seem to me to be so easy, to obtain honour from those northerners.
Fréttist mér og svo til sem maðurinn muni þar niður kominn að ekki muni hægt eftir að leita".	Reported me and so to that the-man should there down come that not should possible after to seek".	It has been reported to me that this man has gone down somewhere that it will not be possible to seek him out.
Bolli tók þó við málinu um síðir og fór Guðrún norður og kom heim.	Bolli took though with the-case about eventually and travelled Gudrun north and came home.	Bolli agreed to take on the case, and Gudrun travelled north and came home.
Hún sagði Þórði bónda sínum svo sem nú var komið og líður nú svo fram um hríð.	She told Thord husband hers so as now was come and passed so from about awhile.	When she arrived home, she told her husband Thord what had happened, and so it passed for a while.
Eftir jól um veturinn var lagður fundur í Skagafirði að Þverá og stefndi Þorvaldur þangað Guðdala-Starra.	After Yule about winter was laid a-meeting in Skagafjord at Thvera and summoned Thorvald from-there Starri-of-Guddalir.	After Yule in winter there was a meeting held in Skagafjord at Thvera, and Thorvald summoned Starri of Guddalir.
Hann var vinur þeirra bræðra.	He was a-friend of-they the-brothers.	He was a friend of the (Hjaltason) brothers.
Þorvaldur fór til þingsins við sína menn og er þeir komu fyrir Urðskriðuhóla þá hljóp úr hlíðinni ofan að þeim maður.	Thorvald travelled to the-assembly with his men and when they came before Urdskriduholar then ran from the-slope down at them a-man.	Thorvald travelled to the assembly with his men, and when they came to Urdskriduholar, a man came running down the slope towards them.
Var þar Þórólfur.	Was it Thorolf.	It was Thorolf.

The Tale of Bolli Bollason (Old Icelandic)

Old Icelandic	Literal	English
Réðst hann í ferð með þeim Þorvaldi.	Rode he in travelling with them Thorvald.	He joined and rode with Thorvald (and his men).
Og er þeir áttu skammt til Þverár þá mælti Þorvaldur við Þórólf:	And when they had a-short-distance to Thvera then spoke Thorvald with Thorolf.	When they had a short distance remaining to Thvera, Thorvald spoke to Thorolf:
"Nú skaltu hafa með þér þrjár merkur silfurs og sitja hér upp frá bænum að Þverá.	"Now shall have with you three marks of-silver and sit here up from farmhouse at Thvera.	"Take three marks of silver and stay here above the farmhouse at Thvera.
Haf það að marki að eg mun snúa skildi mínum og að þér holinu ef þér er frítt og máttu þá fram ganga.	Have this as a-sign that I shall turn shield mine and that you hollow if you are safe and may then from go.	Have this as a sign, that I will turn the inside of my shield if you are safe and can come from there.
Skjöldurinn er hvítur innan".	The-shield is white inside".	The shield is white on the inside".
Og er Þorvaldur kom til þingsins hittust þeir Starri og tóku tal saman.	And when Thorvald came to the-assembly met they Starri and took-to talking together.	And when Thorvald came to the assembly, they met Starri and talked together.
Þorvaldur mælti:	Thorvald spoke.	Thorvald spoke:
"Svo er mál með vexti að eg vil þess beiða að þú takir við Þórólfi stærimanni til varðveislu og trausts.	"So is the-matter with grown that I will this offer that you take with Thorolf Stately-man to hospitality and trust.	"So is the matter has come, I will offer this, that I wish you to take Thorolf Stuck-up into your hospitality and support.
Mun eg fá þér þrjár merkur silfurs og vináttu mína".	Should I fee to-you three marks of-silver and friendship mine".	I shall pay you three marks of silver and give you my friendship.
"Þar er sá maður", svarar Starri, "er mér þykir ekki vinsæll og óvíst að honum fylgi hamingja.	"There is so a-man", answered Starri, "that to-me seems not popular and uncertain that he follows luck.	"There is such a man", answered Starri, "that is not popular in my eyes, and not likely to bring much luck.
En sakir okkars vinskapar þá vil eg við honum taka".	But for-the-sake-of our friendship then will I with him take".	But for the sake of our friendship I will take him with me".
"Þá gerir þú vel", segir Þorvaldur.	"The do you well", said Thorvald.	"You do well in that case", said Thorvald.

The Tale of Bolli Bollason (Old Icelandic)

Old Icelandic	Literal	English
Sneri hann þá skildinum og frá sér hvolfinu og er Þórólfur sér það gengur hann fram og tók Starri við honum.	Turned he then the-shield and from himself half and when Thorolf saw that went he from and took Starri with him.	He then turned his shield from himself half way, and when Thorolf saw that, he went from where he was and received him.
Starri átti jarðhús í Guðdölum því að jafnan voru með honum skógarmenn.	Starri had earth-house in Guddalir because that usually were with him forest-men.	Starri had an earth house in Guddalir because he usually had outlaws with him.
Átti hann og nokkuð sökótt.	Had he also some accusations.	He had also had some charges against him.

3

Bolli Bollason býr til vígsmálið Ólafs.	Bolli Son-of-Bolli prepared to fight-the-case Olaf's.	Bolli Bollason prepared to prosecute Olaf's case.
Hann býst heiman og fer norður til Skagafjarðar við þrjá tigi manna.	He prepared at-home and set-out north to Skagafjord with three ten men.	He made preparations and set out north to Skagafjord with thirty men.
Hann kemur á Miklabæ og er honum þar vel fagnað.	He came to Miklabaer and was he there well welcomed.	He came to Miklabaer and was well welcomed there.
Segir hann hversu af stóð um ferðir hans:	Said he how-so of stood about journey his.	He told them the reasons for his journey.
"Ætla eg að hafa fram vígsmálið nú á Hegranessþingi á hendur Þórólfi stærimanni.	"Intend I to have from fight-the-case now to Hegranes-Assembly in hand Thorolf Stately-man.	"I intend to prosecute the case at Hegranes Assembly for Thorolf Stuck-up.
Vildi eg að þú værir mér um þetta mál liðsinnaður".	Wish I that you would-be to-me about this matter team-minded".	I would like you to assist and cooperate with me in this matter".
Arnór svarar:	Arnor answered.	Arnor answered:
"Ekki þykir mér þú Bolli vænt stefna út er þú sækir norður hingað, við slíka ójafnaðarmenn sem hér er að eiga.	"Not seems to-me you Bolli expect agreement from that you seek north here, with such un-equal-men which here are to in.	"It doesn't seems to me, Bolli, that you can expect an agreement that you seek here in the north, with such unjust men that are here".
Munu þeir þetta mál meir verja með kappi en réttindum.	Should they this matter more protect with warriors whether right.	They would defend this matter as warriors whether just or unjust.

The Tale of Bolli Bollason (Old Icelandic)

Old Icelandic	Literal	English
En ærin nauðsyn þykir mér þér á vera.	But considerable necessity seems to-me to-you to be.	But it seems that you have a considerable necessity.
Munum vér og freista að þetta mál gangi fram".	Should we also try that this matter going from".	So we should try to do what we can in this matter.
Arnór dregur að sér fjölmenni mikið.	Arnor drew to himself followers-many much.	Arnor collected a large number of men.
Ríða þeir Bolli til þingsins.	Rode they Bolli to the-assembly.	They rode with Bolli to the assembly.
Þeir bræður fjölmenna mjög til Hegranesþings.	The brothers following-men much to Hegranes-Assembly.	The brothers also came with many followers to Hegranes Assembly.
Þeir hafa frétt um ferðir Bolla.	They had news about journey Bolli's.	They had news about Bolli's journey.
Ætla þeir að verja málið.	Intended they to defend the-case.	They intended to defend the case.
Og er menn koma til þingsins hefir Bolli fram sakir á hendur Þórólfi.	And when people came to the-assembly had Bolli from the-charges in hand Thorolf.	And when people came to the assembly, Bolli presented the charges against Thorolf,
Og er til varna var boðið gengu þeir til Þorvaldur og Starri við sveit sína og hugðu að eyða málinu fyrir Bolla með styrk og ofríki.	And was to defence was bid went they to Thorvald and Starri with company theirs and thought that devastate the-case before Bolli with strength and un-rule.	and then the defence was made, and Thorvald and Starri came forward with their company, they intended to block Bolli's prosecution with strength and unruliness.
En er þetta sér Arnór gengur hann í milli með sína sveit og mælti:	Then when this saw Arnor went he in between with his company and spoke.	Then when Arnor saw this, he went in-between with his company and spoke:
"Það er mönnum einsætt að færa hér eigi svo marga góða menn í vandræði sem á horfist að menn skuli eigi ná lögum um mál sín.	"It is to-people one-agreement that bringing here not so many good men in dispute as to looks that people shall not obtain law about the-matter this.	"It is clear that so many good men should not be here in the dispute as now looks likely, that people shall not get justice in this matter.
Er og ófallið að fylgja Þórólfi um þetta mál.	It-is also misguided to follow Thorolf about this case.	It is also misguided to support Thorolf in this case.

The Tale of Bolli Bollason (Old Icelandic)

Old Icelandic	Literal	English
Muntu Þorvaldur og óliðdrjúgur verða ef reyna skal".	Should-you Thorvald also un-substantial-company become if tested shall-be".	And you, Thorvald, will have little backing if it comes to a show of force.
Þeir Þorvaldur og Starri sáu nú að málið mundi fram ganga því að þeir höfðu ekki liðsafla við þeim Arnóri og léttu þeir frá.	They Thorvald and Starri saw now that the-case should from go since that they had not company-provided with them Arnor and relieved they from.	Thorvald and Starri now saw that the case would be concluded, since they did not have the same number of men with them to match Arnor, so they withdrew.
Bolli sekti Þórólf stærimann þar á Hegranessþingi um víg Ólafs frænda síns og fór við það heim.	Bolli convicted Thorolf Stately-man there at Hegranes-Assembly about the-killing-of Olaf's kinsman his and travelled with that home.	Bolli convicted Thorolf Stuck-up there at Hegranes Assembly for the killing of his kinsman Olaf, and then went home.
Skildust þeir Arnór með kærleikum.	Separated they Arnor with friendship.	He separated from Arnor with friendship.
Sat Bolli í búi sínu.	Sat Bolli in farm his.	Bolli stayed on his farm.

4

Þorgrímur hét maður.	Thorgrim was-named a-man.	There was a man named Thorgrim.
Hann átti skip uppi standanda í Hrútafirði.	He had a-ship up stood in Hrutafjord.	He had a ship which stood at Hrutafjord.
Þangað reið Starri og Þórólfur við honum.	There rode Starri and Thorolf to him.	Starri and Thorolf rode there to be with him.
Starri mælti við stýrimann:	Starri spoke with the-captain.	Starri spoke with the captain:
"Hér er maður að eg vil að þú takir við og flytjir utan og hér eru þrjár merkur silfurs er þú skalt hafa og þar með vináttu mína".	"Here is a-man that I wish that you take with and with-fleetness abroad and here are three marks of-silver and you shall have also there with friendship mine".	"Here is a man that I wish you to take abroad quickly, and here are three marks of silver, and you shall also have my friendship".
Þorgrímur mælti:	Thorgrim spoke.	Thorgrim spoke:
"Á þessu þykir mér nokkur vandi hversu af hendi verður leyst.	"About this seems to-me somewhat difficulty how-so of hand becomes solved.	"It seems to me that it will be somewhat difficult to be able to solve.

The Tale of Bolli Bollason (Old Icelandic)

Old Icelandic	Literal	English
En við áskoran þína mun eg við honum taka.	But with challenge yours should I with him take.	But with your challenge I shall take him,
En þó þykir mér þessi maður vera ekki giftuvænlegur".	But though seems to-me this a-man becomes not luck-promised".	though it seems to me that this man promises much luck".
Þórólfur réðst nú í sveit með kaupmönnum en Starri ríður heim við svo búið.	Thorolf rode now in company with trading-men and Starri rode home with so prepared.	Thorolf then rode in company with the merchants, and Starri rode home so prepared.
Nú er að segja frá Bolla.	Now is to say from Bolli.	Now the story turns to Bolli.
Hann hugsar nú efni þeirra Þórólfs og þykir eigi verða mjög með öllu fylgt ef Þórólfur skal sleppa.	He thought now the-matter theirs Thorolf's and thought not would-be much with all followed if Thorolf should escape.	He thought about their matter with Thorolf and thought it would not be much if it followed that Thorolf should escape.
Frétti hann nú að hann er til skips ráðinn.	Learned he now that he was to ships riding.	He now learned that he was riding to the ships.
Bolli býst heiman.	Bolli prepared from-home.	Bolli prepared to leave home.
Setur hann hjálm á höfuð sér, skjöld á hlið.	Set he helmet on head his, shield about side.	He put his helmet on his head, his shield by his side,
Spjót hafði hann í hendi en gyrður sverðinu Fótbít.	Spear had he in hand in buckled the-sword Leg-Biter.	his spear in his hand, and buckled the sword Leg Biter.
Hann ríður norður til Hrútafjarðar og kom í það mund er kaupmenn voru albúnir.	He rode north to Hrutafjord and came in so about-that-time as trading-men were all-prepared.	He rode north to Hrutafjord and arrived at about the time that the merchants were all prepared.
Var þá og vindur á kominn.	Then when also the-wind up came.	Then the wind also came up.
Og er Bolli reið að búðardyrunum gekk Þórólfur út í því og hafði húðfat í fangi sér.	And as Bolli rode to the-booth-doors went Thorolf out about because also had bed-roll in arms his.	And as Bolli rode up to the camp doors, Thorolf came out carrying his bed roll in his arms.
Bolli bregður Fótbít og leggur í gegnum hann.	Bolli drew Leg-Biter and lunged at through him.	Bolli drew Leg Biter and lunged through him.
Fellur Þórólfur á bak aftur í búðina inn en Bolli hleypur á hest sinn.	Fell Thorolf on back down in the-booth inside and Bolli ran to horse his.	Thorolf fell back into the camp, and Bolli ran to his horse.

The Tale of Bolli Bollason (Old Icelandic)

Old Icelandic	Literal	English
Kaupmenn hljópu saman og að honum.	Trading-men ran together and at him.	The merchants ran together towards him.
Bolli mælti:	Bolli spoke.	Bolli spoke:
"Hitt er yður ráðlegast að láta nú vera kyrrt því að yður mun ofstýri verða að leggja mig við velli.	"Find is you advisable that leave now being peace because that you should unmanageable being to lay me with the-fields.	"It is advisable that you leave now in peace, because you shall not manage to bring me down in the fields,
En vera má að eg kvisti einnhvern yðvarn eða alla tvo áður eg er felldur".	But being may that I trim one of-you or all two before I am falling".	and it may be, that I trim one or two of you before I fall".
Þorgrímur svarar:	Thorgrim said.	Thorgrim said:
"Eg hygg að þetta sé satt".	"I think that this is true".	"I think that this is true".
Létu þeir vera kyrrt en Bolli reið heim og hefir sótt mikinn frama í þessi ferð.	Let they be still and Bolli rode home and had attended much honour in this journey.	They remained still, and Bolli rode home and earned a great deal of honour from this journey.
Fær hann af þessu virðing mikla og þótti mönnum farið skörulega, hefir sektan manninn í öðrum fjórðungi en síðan riðið einn saman í hendur óvinum sínum og drepið hann þar.	Accomplished he of this honour much and thought people travelled boldly, had outlawed person in another district and then ride alone together in hand un-friends his and kill him there.	He accomplished much honour in this, and people thought he travelled boldly, to have the man outlawed in another district, and then riding alone into the hands of his enemies and killing him there.

5

Um sumarið á alþingi fundust þeir Bolli og Guðmundur hinn ríki og töluðu margt.	About summer at the-assembly met they Bolli and Gudmund the powerful and talked much.	About summer at the assembly Bolli and Gudmund the Powerful met and talked much.
Þá mælti Guðmundur:	Then spoke Gudmund.	Then Gudmund spoke:
"Því vil eg lýsa Bolli að eg vil við slíka menn vingast sem þér eruð.	"Because wish I show Bolli that I wish with such people make-friends as you are.	"I wish to say to you, Bolli, that I wish to make friends with people like you.
Eg vil bjóða þér norður til mín til hálfs mánaðar veislu og þykir mér betur að þú komir".	I wish to-invite you north to mine to half-month's a-month's feast and consider me better that you come".	I wish to invite you north to mine for a half month's feast, and I would think the best of it if you came".

The Tale of Bolli Bollason (Old Icelandic)

Old Icelandic	Literal	English
Bolli svarar, að vísu vill hann þiggja sæmdir að slíkum manni og hét hann ferðinni.	Bolli answered, that certainly wished he accept honour from such a-man and promised he the-journey.	Bolli answered that he certainly wished to accept this honour from such a man, and promised that he would make the journey.
Þá urðu og fleiri menn til að veita honum þessi vinganarmál.	Then became also more men to that grant him this friendship-matter.	Then others also came to grant him friendship.
Arnór kerlingarnef bauð Bolla og til veislu á Miklabæ.	Arnor Crone's-nose invited Bolli also to feast at Miklabaer.	Arnor Crone's-Nose also invited Bolli to a feast at Miklabaer.
Maður hét Þorsteinn.	A-man named Thorstein.	There was a man named Thorstein.
Hann bjó að Hálsi.	He lived at Hals.	He lived at Hals.
Hann var sonur Hellu-Narfa.	He was the-son-of Hellu-Narfi.	He was the son of Hellu-Narfi.
Hann bauð Bolla til sín er hann færi norðan og Þórður af Marbæli bauð Bolla.	He invited Bolli to his that he travel north and Thord at Marbaeli invited Bolli.	He invited Bolli to travel north to his, and so did Thord at Marbaeli.
Fóru menn af þinginu og reið Bolli heim.	Travelled people to the-assembly and rode Bolli home.	People travelled to the assembly, and Bolli rode home.
Þetta sumar kom skip í Dögurðarnes og settist þar upp.	That summer came a-ship in Dagverdarnes and set there up.	That summer a ship came in at Dagverdarnes and set up there.
Bolli tók til vistar í Tungu tólf kaupmenn.	Bolli took to lodging at Tunga twelve trading-men.	Bolli took lodging for twelve trading men.
Voru þeir þar um veturinn og veitti Bolli þeim allstórmannlega.	Were they there about winter and granted Bolli home all-great-man-like.	They were there about winter, and Bolli provided from them generously.
Sátu þeir um kyrrt fram yfir jól.	Sat they about still from over Yule.	They stayed there for Yule.
En eftir jól ætlar Bolli að vitja heimboðanna norður og lætur hann þá járna hesta og býr ferð sína.	Then after Yule intended Bolli to visit home-invitation north and had he then iron-shod horses and prepared travel his.	Then after Yule, Bolli intended to visit the north as invited, and he had horses shod and prepared to travel.
Voru þeir átján í reið.	Were they eighteen in riding.	There were eighteen of them riding.

The Tale of Bolli Bollason (Old Icelandic)

Old Icelandic	Literal	English
Voru kaupmenn allir vopnaðir.	Were trading-men all weaponed.	All the merchants were armed.
Bolli reið í blárri kápu og hafði í hendi spjótið konungsnaut hið góða.	Bolli rode in black cape and had in hand spear king's-gift the good.	Bolli rode in a black cape and in his hand the spear, King's Gift, the good.
Þeir ríða nú norður og koma á Marbæli til Þórðar.	They rode now north and came to Marbaeli to Thord.	They now rode north and came to Marbaeli to Thord.
Var þar allvel við þeim tekið, sátu þrjár nætur í miklum fagnaði.	Were there all-well with them taken, sat three nights in much celebration.	They were all well received and stayed three nights in celebration.
Þaðan riðu þeir á Miklabæ til Arnórs og tók hann ágætlega vel við þeim.	From-there rode they to Miklabaer to Arnor's and took him greatly well with them.	From there they rode to Miklabaer to Arnor, and he received them well.
Var þar veisla hin besta.	Was there the-feast the best.	There was the best feast.
Þá mælti Arnór:	Then spoke Arnor.	Then Arnor spoke:
"Vel hefir þú gert Bolli er þú hefir mig heimsótt.	"Well have you done Bolli that you have my home-sought.	"You have done well, Bolli, for seeking my home.
Þykir mér þú hafa lýst í því við mig mikinn félagsskap.	Think I you have shown it therefore with me much comradeship.	I think you have therefore shown me much comradeship.
Skulu eigi eftir betri gjafir með mér en þú skalt þiggja mega.	Shall not after better gifts with me than you shall accept may.	And no better gifts will remain here with me that the ones you accept at parting.
Mín vinátta skal þér og heimul vera.	My friendship shall to-you also have-right be.	My friendship is also yours for the asking.
En nokkur grunur er mér á að þér séu eigi allir menn vinhollir í þessu héraði, þykjast sviptir vera sæmdum.	But somewhat suspect that for-me about that you being not all men open-whole in this district, think loss being honour.	But I suspect that around me, not everyone in this district is inclined towards you, thinking that they have lost their honour.
Kemur það mest til þeirra Hjaltasona.	Coming that most to they Hjaltasons.	Most of that coming to the Hjaltasons.
Mun eg nú ráðast til ferðar með þér norður á Heljardalsheiði þá er þér farið héðan".	Should I now arrange to travel with you north to Heljardal Heath then when you travel from-here".	I shall now arrange to travel north with you to Herjardal Heath when you leave here".

The Tale of Bolli Bollason (Old Icelandic)

Old Icelandic	Literal	English
Bolli svarar:	Bolli answered.	Bolli answered:
"Þakka vil eg yður Arnór bóndi alla sæmd er þér gerið til mín nú og fyrrum.	"Thanks wish I you Arnor host all honour that you do about mine now and before-us.	"I wish to thank you, Arnor my host, for all the honour, that you have shown me now before us.
Þykir mér og það bæta vorn flokk að þér ríðið með oss.	Seems to-me also that better our flock that you ride with us.	It seems to me better for our flock, if you ride with us.
En allt hugðum vér að fara með spekt um þessi héruð.	Then all think we that travel with wisdom about this district.	Then we think we will travel with wisdom through this district,
En ef aðrir leita á oss þá má vera að vér leikum þá enn nokkuð í mót".	That if others look for us then may be that we sport then but somewhat in meeting".	so that if others look for us, as they may, then we will give them some sport in meeting us".
Síðan ræðst Arnór til ferðar með þeim og ríða nú veg sinn.	Afterwards rode Arnor to travel with them and rode now way theirs.	Afterwards Arnor prepared to ride with them, and they set out on their way.

6

Nú er að segja frá Þorvaldi að hann tekur til orða við Þórð bróður sinn:	Now is to say from Thorvald that he took to words with Thord brother his.	Now the story turns to Thorvald, that he spoke to his brother Thord:
"Vita muntu að Bolli fer héðra að heimboðum.	"Know shall-you that Bolli travels district at home-invitations.	"You know that Bolli travels in this district going to home invitations.
Eru þeir nú að Arnórs átján saman og ætla norður Heljardalsheiði".	Are they now at Arnor's eighteen together and intend north Heljardal Heath".	There are eighteen of then together, and they intend north to Herjardal Heath.
"Veit eg það", svarar Þórður.	"Know I that", answered Thord.	"I know that", answered Thord.
Þorvaldur mælti:	Thorvald spoke.	Thorvald said:
"Ekki er mér þó um það að Bolli hlaupi hér svo um horn oss að vér finnum hann eigi því að eg veit eigi hver minni sæmd hefir meir niður drepið en hann".	"Not am I though about that that Bolli running here so about horn ours that we find him not such that I know none who diminish honour has more down killing than him".	"I am not happy with the idea that Bolli is running around here under our noses, and we don't go to meet him, because I know no one, who has diminished my honour more than him".
Þórður mælti:	Thord spoke.	Thord spoke:

The Tale of Bolli Bollason (Old Icelandic)

Old Icelandic	Literal	English
"Mjög ertu íhlutunarsamur og meir en eg vildi og ófarin mundi þessi ef eg réði.	"Great are-you in-sharing-together also more than I wish and un-faring should this if I decide.	"You are great at sharing in things more than I wish, and this should not go, if I am the one to decide.
Þykir mér óvíst að Bolli sé ráðlaus fyrir þér".	Seems to-me uncertain that Bolli so ill-advised for you".	It seems uncertain to me, that Bolli would be so ill-advised about you".
"Eigi mun eg letjast láta", svarar Þorvaldur, "en þú munt ráða ferð þinni".	"Not should I dissuaded allow", answered Thorvald, "but you should decide travel yours".	"I should not allow that to dissuade me", answered Thorvald, "but you should decide your course".
Þórður mælti:	Thord spoke.	Third spoke:
"Eigi mun eg eftir sitja ef þú ferð bróðir en þér munum vér eigna alla virðing þá er vér hljótum í þessi ferð, og svo ef öðruvís ber til".	"Not should I after sitting if you travel brother but you shall we own all worthiness then as we we-get in this journey, and so if other-knowing bear to".	"I shall not stay, if you travel, brother, but you shall own all the honour we may get from this journey, or any other consequences".
Þorvaldur safnar að sér mönnum og verða þeir átján saman og ríða á leið fyrir þá Bolla og ætla að sitja fyrir þeim.	Thorvald collected for his men and became they eighteen together and rode to journey for then Bolli and intended to sit before them.	Thorvald collected together his men to become a party of eighteen and together they rode on the journey that Bolli made and intended to sit in ambush before them.
Þeir Arnór og Bolli ríða nú með sína menn	They Arnor and Bolli rode now with their men	Arnor and Bolli rode with their men.
og er skammt var í milli þeirra og Hjaltasona þá mælti Bolli til Arnórs:	and when short-distance were in between them and Hjaltasons then spoke Bolli to Arnor's.	And when there was a short distance between them and the Hjaltasons, Bolli said to Arnor:
"Mun eigi það nú ráð að þér hverfið aftur? Hafið þér þó fylgt oss hið drengilegsta.	"Should not is now advised that you turn back?" Have you though followed us the bravely.	"Should it not now be advised that you turn back? Though you have followed us bravely.
Munu þeir Hjaltasynir ekki sæta fláráðum við mig".	Should they Hjaltasons not sit-in-ambush treacherous with me".	The Hjaltasons should not sit in ambush for me in treachery".
Arnór mælti:	Arnor spoke.	Arnor spoke:

The Tale of Bolli Bollason (Old Icelandic)

Old Icelandic	Literal	English
"Eigi mun eg enn aftur hverfa því að svo er sem annar segi mér að Þorvaldur muni til þess ætla að hafa fund þinn.	"Not should I then back turn because that so is that another say me that Thorvald should to this intend to have meet you.	"I shall not turn back, because something tells me that Thorvald intends to meet you,
Eða hvað sé eg þar upp koma, blika þar eigi skildir við? Og munu þar vera Hjaltasynir.	And what see I there up coming, shining there not shields with?" And should there be Hjaltasons.	and what is that I see moving there? Is that not the glimmer of shields? That will be the Hjaltasons.
En þó mætti nú svo um búast að þessi þeirra ferð yrði þeim til engrar virðingar en megi metast fjörráð við þig".	But though may now so about prepare that this they travel with them to no honour but may meet plotting against you".	But now shall we be prepared, that they will travel with no honour, that they are plotting against you".
Nú sjá þeir Þorvaldur bræður að þeir Bolli eru hvergi liðfærri en þeir og þykjast sjá ef þeir sýna nokkura óhæfu af sér að þeirra kostur mundi mikið versna.	Now saw they Thorvald brothers that they Bolli were neither company-less than they and realised saw if they seemed somewhat unqualified of themselves that they chose would much worse.	Thorvald and his brother saw that Bolli and his company were no less in numbers than they were, and when they saw this they realised, that if they were unqualified themselves, that the choice of aggression would be much worse.
Sýnist þeim það ráðlegast að snúa aftur alls þeir máttu ekki sínum vilja fram koma.	Seemed to-them that advice that return back all they may not theirs will from coming.	It seemed to them that the best advice was now to turn back, since they were not able to carry out their will.
Þá mælti Þórður:	Then spoke Thord.	Then Thord spoke:
"Nú fór sem mig varði að þessi ferð mundi verða hæðileg og þætti mér enn betra heima setið.	"Now goes as much expect that this journey would become mockery and seems to-me the better home stay.	"Now it goes as I expected, that this journey would make a mockery of us, and it seems better if we had stayed at home,
Höfum sýnt oss í fjandskap við menn en komið engu á leið".	Has shown us in fiendship with people but come nothing from passed".	we have shown hostility with people, but achieved nothing".
Þeir Bolli ríða leið sína.	They Bolli rode way theirs.	Bolli and his men rode their way.
Fylgir Arnór þeim upp á heiðina og skildi hann eigi fyrr við þá en hallaði af norður.	Followed Arnor them up to the-heath and separated he not before with then but turned of north.	Arnor followed them up to the heath, and did not leave them until they turned north.

The Tale of Bolli Bollason (Old Icelandic)

Old Icelandic	Literal	English
Þá hvarf hann aftur en þeir riðu ofan eftir Svarfaðardal og komu á bæ þann er á Skeiði heitir.	Then broke-away he back but they rode down along Svarfadardal and came to a-farm then which was Skeid named.	Then he broke away and returned home while they rode down through Svarfadardal until they reached a farm called Skeid.
Þar bjó sá maður er Helgi hét.	There lived so a-man who Helgi named.	There lived a man there who was named Helgi.
Hann var ættsmár og illa í skapi, auðigur að fé.	He was of-family-small and bad in mood, rich in wealth.	He was not from a good family, ill-tempered, but wealthy.
Hann átti þá konu er Sigríður hét.	He had then wife who Sigrid named.	He had a wife named Sigrid.
Hún var frændkona Þorsteins Hellu-Narfasonar.	She was kinswoman Thorstein's Hellu-Narfason.	The was a kinswoman of Thorstein Hellu-Narfason.
Hún var þeirra skörungur meiri.	She was of-them noble the-more.	She was the more outstanding of them.
Þeir Bolli litu heygarð hjá sér.	There Bolli looked hay-stacks beside them.	Bolli looked and saw hay stacks nearby.
Stigu þeir þar af baki og kasta þeir fyrir hesta sína og verja til heldur litlu en þó hélt Bolli þeim aftur að heygjöfinni.	Dismounted they there off horseback and cast there before horses theirs and guarding to rather little but though held Bolli they back the hay-giving.	They dismounted their horses, and cast them before the horses, taking rather little, and Bolli restrained them even more.
"Veit eg eigi", segir hann, "hvert skaplyndi bóndi hefir".	"Know I not", said he, "what nature the-farmer has".	"I don't know", he said, "what sort of nature this farmer has".
Þeir gáfu heyvöndul og létu hestana grípa í.	They gave hay-bundle and led the-horses grab to.	They took handfuls of hay and let the horses eat them.
Á bænum heima gekk út maður og þegar inn aftur og mælti:	About the-farm home went out a-man and from-there inside returned and spoke.	About the farm came out a man from inside who went back inside and spoke:
"Menn eru við heygarð þinn bóndi og reyna desjarnar".	"Men are with hay-stacks yours farmer and trying the-hay".	"Men are at your haystacks, master, trying the hay".
Sigríður húsfreyja svarar:	Sigrid housewife answered.	Sigrid the housewife answered,
"Þeir einir munu þar menn vera að það mun ráð að spara eigi hey við".	"They only would there men be that it would decide to spare not hey with".	"The only men who will be there, are those that it will be a good idea not to spare hay".

The Tale of Bolli Bollason (Old Icelandic)

Old Icelandic	Literal	English
Helgi hljóp upp í óðafári og kvað aldrei hana skyldu þessu ráða að hann léti stela heyjum sínum.	Helgi leapt up in a-hurry and said never he should this allow that he let steal hay his.	Helgi leapt up in a hurry and said that he would never allow others to steal his hay.
Hann hleypur þegar sem hann sé vitlaus og kemur þar að sem þeir áðu.	He ran immediately as-if he was wit-less and came there to as they to.	He ran out immediately as if he were crazed, and came up to where the men were.
Bolli stóð upp er hann leit ferðina mannsins og studdist við spjótið konungsnaut.	Bolli stood up as he saw going the-man and stood with the-spear king's-gift.	Bolli stood up as he saw the man coming, and stood up with the help of the spear, King's Gift.
Og þegar Helgi kom að honum mælti hann:	And as-soon-as Helgi came to him spoke he.	As soon as Helgi reached him, he spoke:
"Hverjir eru þessir þjófarnir er mér bjóða ofríki og stela mig eign minni og rífa í sundur hey mitt fyrir faraskjóta sína?"	"Who are these thieves that me offer unruly and stealing my own less and tearing to asunder hay mine for horses theirs?"	"Who are these thieves, that harass me and steal what is mine and tearing apart my hay for their horses?".
Bolli segir nafn sitt.	Bolli said name his.	Bolli told him his name.
Helgi svarar:	Helgi answered.	Helgi answered:
"Það er óliðlegt nafn og muntu vera óréttvís".	"That is unsuitable name and should-you be un-right-knowing".	"That is an unsuitable name, and you must be an unjust man".
"Vera má að svo sé", segir Bolli, "en hinu skaltu mæta er réttvísi er í".	"Be-it may that so this", said Bolli, "but the shall-you meet which right-knowing that is".	"It may be that it is", said Bolli, "but you shall have your justice".
Bolli keyrði þá hestana frá heyinu og bað þá eigi æja lengur.	Bolli spurred then horses from the-hay and ordered then none rest any-longer.	Bolli then spurred the horses away from the hay, and ordered that none would rest there any longer.
Helgi mælti:	Helgi spoke.	Helgi spoke:
"Eg kalla yður hafa stolið mig þessu sem þér hafið haft og gert á hendur yður skóggangssök".	"I declare you have stolen mine this as you have had and done in hand your forest-seeking".	"I declare you have stolen what is mine, which you have, and you have committed an offence to outlawry".

The Tale of Bolli Bollason (Old Icelandic)

Old Icelandic	Literal	English
"Þú munt vilja bóndi", sagði Bolli, "að vér komum fyrir oss fébótum við þig og hafir þú eigi sakir á oss.	"You should wish farmer", said Bolli, "that we come before us compensation with you and have you no conviction of us.	"You will want, farmer", said Bolli, "that we bring forth compensation with you, so that you will have no conviction with us.
Mun eg gjalda tvenn verð fyrir hey þitt".	Shall I pay twice the-worth for hay yours".	I shall pay twice the worth of your hay".
"Það fer heldur fjarri", svarar hann, "mun eg framar á hyggja um það er vér skiljum".	"That goes behind far-away", answered he, "should I honour to think about that which our understanding".	"That is nowhere near enough", he answered, "I should think about my honour, what understanding we shall have".
Bolli mælti:	Bolli spoke.	Bolli spoke:
"Eru nokkurir hlutir þeir bóndi er þú viljir hafa í sætt af oss?"	"Are-there some things they farmer that you wish to-have to settle of us?"	"Are there any objects, farmer, that you wish to have to settle with us?".
"Það þykir mér vera mega", svarar Helgi, "að eg vilji spjót það hið gullrekna er þú hefir í hendi".	"That think I be may", answered Helgi, "that I wish spear that the gold-inlaid that you have in hand".	"I think it might be", answered Helgi, "that I wish to have the spear that is inlaid with gold, that you have in your hand".
"Eigi veit eg", sagði Bolli, "hvort eg nenni það til að láta.	"Not know I", said Bolli, "whether I care that to have allow.	"I do not know", said Bolli, "whether I care to allow that.
Hefi eg annað nokkuð heldur fyrir því ætlað.	Have I another something rather for therefore intended.	I have some other intentions with it.
Máttu það og varla tala að beiðast vopns úr hendi mér.	May that also barely speak to ask weapons from-out-of hand mine.	You could hardly speak to ask for a weapon from my hand.
Tak heldur annað fé svo mikið að þú þykist vel haldinn af".	Take rather another fee so much that you think well holds of".	Take instead as much money as you consider that you are well off".
"Fjarri fer það", svarar Helgi, "er það og best að þér svarið slíku fyrir sem þér hafið til gert".	"Far-away goes that", answered Helgi, "is it also best that you answer such for as you have to done".	"Far be it from me", answered Helgi, "it is best that you answer for what you have done".
Síðan hóf Helgi upp stefnu og stefndi Bolla um þjófnað og lét varða skóggang.	Then began Helgi upped summons and charged Bolli with theft and had warranted outlawry.	Then Helgi started a lawsuit and sued Bolli for theft and had a warranted outlawry.

The Tale of Bolli Bollason (Old Icelandic)

Old Icelandic	Literal	English
Bolli stóð og heyrði til og brosti við lítinn þann.	Bolli stood and heard to and laughed against a-little then.	Bolli stood and listened and laughed a little.
En er Helgi hafði lokið stefnunni mælti hann:	Then when Helgi had finished the-summons spoke he.	But when Helgi had finished the summons, he said:
"Nær fórstu heiman?"	"When travelled-you from-home?"	"When did you leave home?".
Bolli sagði honum.	Bolli told him.	Bolli told him.
Þá mælti bóndi:	Then spoke the-farmer.	Then the farmer said:
"Þá tel eg þig hafa á öðrum alist meir en hálfan mánuð".	"Then say I you have of others homes more than half a-month".	"Then I think you have been living off others for more than half a month".
Helgi hefur þá upp aðra stefnu og stefnir Bolla um verðgang.	Helgi had then upped another summons and charged Bolli with vagrancy.	Helgi had then brought up another summons and charged Bolli with vagrancy.
Og er því var lokið þá mælti Bolli:	And when that was finished then spoke Bolli.	And when it was over, Bolli said:
"Þú hefir mikið við Helgi og mun betur fallið að leika nokkuð í móti við þig".	"You have much with Helgi and should better make that sport somewhat in meeting with you".	"You are making a lot of it, Helgi, and it would be better to play something against you".
Þá hefur Bolli upp stefnu og stefndi Helga um illmæli við sig og annarri stefnu um brekráð til fjár síns.	Then had Bolli upped summons and charged Helgi about slander with him and another summons about treachery to wealth his.	Then Bolli instituted a summons, and sued Helgi for a slander against him, and another summons for accusations of treachery to his property.
Þeir mæltu förunautar hans að drepa skyldi skelmi þann.	There spoke companions his that kill should devilish-man then.	They, his companions, said that the scoundrel should be killed.
Bolli kvað það eigi skyldu.	Bolli said that not should.	Bolli said it was not his duty.
Bolli lét varða skóggang.	Bolli had warranted outlawry.	Bolli had warranted outlawry.
Hann mælti eftir stefnuna:	He spoke after the-summons.	He said after the summons:

The Tale of Bolli Bollason (Old Icelandic)

Old Icelandic	Literal	English
"Þér skuluð færa heim húsfreyju Helga hníf og belti er eg sendi henni því að mér er sagt að hún hafi gott eina lagt til vorra haga".	"You should bring home housewife Helgi knife and belt that I send her because to me is said that she had benefit one had to ours fairly".	"You should bring home this knife and belt for your housewife that I send her, because I am told that she spoke up fairly for us".
Bolli ríður nú í brott en Helgi er þar eftir.	Bolli rode now to away then Helgi was there afterwards.	Bolli now rode away, and Helgi was left behind.
Þeir Bolli koma til Þorsteins á Háls og fá þar góðar viðtökur.	They Bolli came to Thorstein's at Hals and got there good withtaken.	Bolli and his men came to Thorstein at Hals and were well received there.
Er þar búin veisla fríð.	As there prepared feast peaceful.	There was a beautiful feast there.

7

Old Icelandic	Literal	English
Nú er að segja frá Helga að hann kemur heim á Skeið og segir húsfreyju sinni hvað þeir Bolli höfðu við ást.	Now is it to-say from Helgi that he came home at Skeid and told housewife his what they Bolli had with to.	Now it is said of Helgi that he came home to Skeid and told his housewife what Bolli and they had done.
"Þykist eg eigi vita", segir hann, "hvað mér verður til ráðs að eiga við slíkan mann sem Bolli er en eg er málamaður engi.	"Think I not know", said he, "what to-me becomes to advice that have with such men as Bolli is nor I am man-of-law none.	"I do not think I know", he said, "what I can do with such a man as Bolli is, nor am I a lawyer.
Á eg og ekki marga þá er mér muni að málum veita".	As I also not many then that me would to the-matter grant".	I also do not have many who will help me".
Sigríður húsfreyja svarar:	Sigrid housewife answered.	Sigrid the housewife answered:
"Þú ert orðinn mannfóli mikill, hefir átt við hina göfgustu menn og gert þig að undri.	"You have become an-idiot much, have had with these noblest men and made you a fool-of-yourself.	"You have been very foolish, you have dealt with these noblest men, and you have made a fool of yourself.
Mun þér og fara sem maklegt er að þú munt hér fyrir upp gefa allt fé þitt og sjálfan þig".	Should you also go as deserve then that you should here because-of up give all wealth yours and yourself you".	It will be as you deserve, that you shall lose your wealth and your life".

The Tale of Bolli Bollason (Old Icelandic)

Old Icelandic	Literal	English
Helgi heyrði á orð hennar og þóttu ill vera en grunaði þó að satt mundi vera því að honum var svo farið að hann var vesalmenni og þó skapillur og heimskur.	Helgi heard the words hers and thought ill were but suspected though that true would be because that he was so fared that cowardly was wretch and though bad-temper and foolishness.	Helgi heard her words, and thought they were evil, but still suspected that it would be true, for he had done so, that he was a poor man, and yet temperamental and foolish.
Sá hann sig engi færi hafa til leiðréttu en mælt sig í ófæru.	Saw he such no way-out had to rectify what talked himself into impassable.	He saw that he had no opportunity to correct himself, the impasse he had talked himself into.
Barst hann heldur illa af fyrir þetta allt jafnsaman.	Overcome he rather ill of for this all together.	He was overcome badly for all of it all at once.
Sigríður lét taka sér hest og reið að finna Þorstein frænda sinn Narfason og voru þeir Bolli þá komnir.	Sigrid had taken her horse and rode to find Thorstein kinsman hers Narfason and were they Bolli then come.	Sigrid had a horse taken, and rode to find Thorstein, her kinsman, Narfason, and Bolli and his men had arrived.
Hún heimti Þorstein á mál og sagði honum í hvert efni komið var.	She asked-for Thorstein to speak-to and told him about how the-matter come was.	She called Thorstein to speak to and told him what had happened.
"Þó hefir slíkt illa til tekist", svarar Þorsteinn.	"Though has such ill to taken", answered Thorstein.	This has turned out very badly", answered Thorstein.
Hún sagði og hversu vel Bolli hafði boðið eða hversu heimsklega Helga fór.	She told also how well Bolli had offered an how-so foolishly Helgi did.	She also said how well Bolli had offered and how stupid Helgi was.
Bað hún Þorstein eiga í allan hlut að þetta mál greiddist.	Asked she Thorstein to-have it all lot that this matter resolved.	She asked Thorstein to have everything to do with this matter being settled.
Eftir það fór hún heim en Þorsteinn kom að máli við Bolla.	After that went she home and Thorstein came to speak with Bolli.	After that she went home, then Thorstein spoke to Bolli:
"Hvað er um vinur", segir hann, "hvort hefir Helgi af Skeiði sýnt fólsku mikla við þig? Vil eg biðja að þér leggið niður fyrir mín orð og virðið það engis því að ómæt eru þar afglapa orð".	"What is about friend", said he, "how has Helgi of Skeid shown falsehood much with you?" Wish I offer that you lay down for my words and honour that none therefore that un-good are there foolish words".	"What is the matter, friend?" he said, "has Helgi of Skeid shown great falsehood to you? I want to ask you to lay down those words and do not honour them, because they are foolish words there".
Bolli svarar:	Bolli answered.	Bolli answers:

The Tale of Bolli Bollason (Old Icelandic)

Old Icelandic	Literal	English
"Það er víst að þetta er engis vert.	"That is certainly that this is none worthy.	"It is certain that this is of no value.
Mun eg mér og ekki um þetta gefa".	Should I to-me also not about this give".	I will not worry about this".
"Þá vil eg", sagði Þorsteinn, "að þér gefið honum upp þetta fyrir mína skyld og hafið þar fyrir mína vináttu".	"Then wish I", said Thorstein, "that you give him up this for my guilt and have there for my friendship".	"Then I wish", said Thorstein, "that you give him this for my sake, and have it there for my friendship".
"Ekki mun þetta til neins voða horfa", sagði Bolli.	"Not would this to any risk turn", said Bolli.	"This will not look to any risk", said Bolli,
"Lét eg mér fátt um finnast og bíður það vordaga".	"Let I me few about encounter and wait to spring-days".	"I did not care much for it, and it will wait for spring days".
Þorsteinn mælti:	Thorstein spoke.	Thorstein said:
"Það mun eg sýna að mér þykir máli skipta að þetta gangi eftir mínum vilja.	"That would I show that to-me thought the-matter exchange that this going after my will.	"I will show that it is important to me that this goes according to my will.
Eg vil gefa þér hest þann er bestur er hér í sveitum og eru tólf saman hrossin".	I will give you horse then the best is here in the-district and there twelve together herd".	I want to give you the horse that is the best here in the countryside, and there are twelve horses together".
Bolli svarar:	Bolli answered.	Bolli answers:
"Slíkt er allvel boðið en eigi þarftu að leggja hér svo mikla stund á.	"Such is all-well offered but not need-you to have here so much while to.	"Such a thing is very well offered, but you do not have to spend so much time here.
Eg gaf mér lítið um slíkt.	I gave me little about such.	I gave myself little of that.
Mun og lítið af verða þá er í dóm kemur".	Should also little of be then that in self-judgement come".	There will be little of it when it comes to judgment".
"Það er sannast", sagði Þorsteinn, "að eg vil selja þér sjálfdæmi fyrir málið".	"That is the-truest", said Thorstein, "that I wish repay you self-judgement for the-matter".	"It is true", said Thorstein, "that I wish to grant you self-judgement in this matter".
Bolli svarar:	Bolli answered.	Bolli answered:

The Tale of Bolli Bollason (Old Icelandic)

Old Icelandic	Literal	English
"Það ætla eg sannast að ekki þurfi um að leitast því að eg vil ekki sættast á þetta mál".	"That expect I truly that no need about to seek because that I wish not reconcile to this case".	"I think it is true that there is no need to seek it, because I do not want to accept a settlement in this matter".
"Þá kýstu það er öllum oss gegnir verst", sagði Þorsteinn,	"Then choosing that which all us serves the-worst", said Thorstein,	"Then you are choosing what is worst for all of us" said Thorstein.
"þótt Helgi sé lítils verður þá er hann þó í venslum bundinn við oss.	"though Helgi is little worth then is he though in marriage bound with us.	"Although Helgi is of little value, he is still bound to us.
Þá munum vér hann eigi upp gefa undir vopn yður síðan þú vilt engis mín orð virða.	Then should we him not up give into weapons yours after you wish none my words value.	Then we will not give him up under your weapons, since you do not want to honour my words.
En að þeim atkvæðum að Helgi hafði í stefnu við þig líst mér það engi sæmdarauki þó að það sé á þing borið".	But that them charges that Helgi has in summoned with you appears to-me that none honour though that it is at the-assembly carried".	But with the charges that Helgi had in summons with you, I do not think it is an honour, even though it has been presented to the assembly".
Skildu þeir Þorsteinn og Bolli heldur fálega.	Separated they Thorstein and Bolli rather poorly.	Thorstein and Bolli parted rather poorly.
Ríður hann í brott og hans félagar og er ekki getið að hann sé með gjöfum í brott leystur.	Rode he to away and his comrades and was not got that he being with gifts in away releasing.	He and his companions rode away, and it is not mentioned that he was released with gifts.

8

Bolli og hans förunautar komu á Möðruvöllu til Guðmundar hins ríka.	Bolli and his companions came to Modruvellir to Gudmund the Powerful.	Bolli and his companions came to Modruvellir to Gudmund the Powerful.
Hann gengur í móti þeim með allri blíðu og var hinn glaðasti.	He came to meet them with all joyfulness and was the gladdest.	He came to meet them with all joyfulness and was the gladdest.
Þar sátu þeir hálfan mánuð í góðum fagnaði.	There stayed they half a-month in good celebration.	They stayed there half a-month in good celebration.
Þá mælti Guðmundur til Bolla:	Then spoke Gudmund to Bolli.	Then Gudmund said to Bolli:

The Tale of Bolli Bollason (Old Icelandic)

Old Icelandic	Literal	English
"Hvað er til haft um það, hefir sundurþykki orðið með yður Þorsteini?"	"What is to have about that, have discord words with your Thorstein?"	"What is that matter, has there been discord with you and Thorstein?"
Bolli kvað lítið til haft um það og tók annað mál.	Bolli spoke little to have about that and took another matter.	Bolli said he had little to say about it and took another matter.
Guðmundur mælti:	Gudmund spoke.	Gudmund said:
"Hverja leið ætlar þú aftur að ríða?"	"What way intend you return to ride?"	"Which way are you going to ride back?"
"Hina sömu", svarar Bolli.	"The same", answered Bolli.	"The same", answered Bolli.
Guðmundur mælti:	Gudmund spoke.	Gudmund said:
"Letja vil eg yður þess því að mér er svo sagt að þið Þorsteinn hafið skilið fálega.	"Discourage wish I you this because that to-me is so said that you Thorstein have separated coldly.	"I wish to discourage you, for I am told that Thorstein has separated with you poorly.
Ver heldur hér með mér og ríð suður í vor og látum þá þessi mál ganga til vegar".	Be rather here with me and ride south in spring and let then this matter go its way".	Stay here with me and ride south in the spring, and then let these matters go".
Bolli lést eigi mundu bregða ferðinni fyrir hót þeirra "en það hugði eg þá er Helgi fólið lét sem heimsklegast og mælti hvert óorðan að öðru við oss og vildi hafa spjótið konungsnaut úr hendi mér fyrir einn heyvöndul að eg skyldi freista að hann fengi ömbun orða sinna.	Bolli said not would break travel for threat theirs "but that think I then that Helgi foolishly had as foolishly and speaking each slanderous to another with us and willing to-have spear king's-gift out-of hand mine for only a-haystack that I should test that he gets return words his.	Bolli said that he would not break from his travel plans because of their threat, "but I think that Helgi was stupid, and spoke foolishly with one slanderous charge after another to us, and wanting to take the spear King's Gift out of my hand for only a haystack, I should see to it that he gets what he deserves for his words.
Hefi eg og annað ætlað fyrir spjótinu að eg mundi heldur gefa þér og þar með gullhringinn þann er stólkonungurinn gaf mér.	Have I also other plans for spear that I should rather give to-you and there with gold-ring then that the-emperor gave me.	I also have other plans for my spear, as I intend to give it to you, along with the gold arm ring that the emperor gave me.
Hygg eg nú að gripirnir séu betur niður komnir en þá að Helgi hefði þá".	Think I now that treasures are better kinsman coming than then that Helgi has then".	I think now, that the treasures are better coming to a kinsman than Helgi having them".

The Tale of Bolli Bollason (Old Icelandic)

Old Icelandic	Literal	English
Guðmundur þakkaði honum gjafir þessar og mælti:	Gudmund thanked him the-gift these and spoke.	Gudmund thanked him for these gifts, and said,
"Hér munu smærri gjafir í móti koma en verðugt er".	"Here shall smaller gifts in return coming than worth are".	"Here smaller gifts will come in return than are worthy".
Guðmundur gaf Bolla skjöld gulllagðan og gullhring og skikkju.	Gudmund gave Bolli shield gold-laid and gold-ring and cloak.	Gudmund gave Bolli a gold-plated shield and a gold ring and a cloak.
Var í henni hið dýrsta klæði og búin öll þar er bæta þótti.	Were about her the dearest clothing and prepared all there was better thought.	And about it was prepared all the most precious material that made it better.
Allir voru gripirnir mjög ágætir.	All were treasures much renowned.	All the treasures were very good.
Þá mælti Guðmundur:	Then spoke Gudmund.	Then Gudmund said:
"Illa þykir mér þú gera Bolli er þú vilt ríða um Svarfaðardal".	"Bad think I you doing Bolli that you wish to-ride about Svarfadardal".	"I think you do badly, Bolli, when you want to ride through Svarfadardal".
Bolli segir það ekki skaða munu.	Bolli said that not scathed would-be.	Bolli said that he would not be scathed.
Riðu þeir í brott og skilja þeir Guðmundur við hinum mestum kærleikum.	Rode they to away and separated they Gudmund with the most friendship.	They rode away, and Gudmund parted with the greatest friendship.
Þeir Bolli ríða nú veg sinn út um Galmarströnd.	Then Bolli rode now way his out about Galmarstrond.	Then Bolli and his men rode their way out over Galmarstrond.
Um kveldið komu þeir á þann bæ er að Krossum heitir.	About evening came they to the farm which that Krossar named.	In the evening they came to a town called Krossar.
Þar bjó sá maður er Óttar hét.	There lived so a-man who Ottar named.	There lived a man named Ottar.
Hann stóð úti.	He stood outside.	He stood outside.
Hann var sköllóttur og í skinnstakki.	He was bald and in skin-cloak.	He was bald, and wearing a fur coat.
Óttar kvaddi þá vel og bauð þeim þar að vera.	Ottar greeted then well and invited them there to be.	Ottar greeted them well and invited them to stay there.
Það þiggja þeir.	That accepted they.	They accepted.

The Tale of Bolli Bollason (Old Icelandic)

Old Icelandic	Literal	English
Var þar góður beini og bóndi hinn kátasti.	Were there good benefit and farmer the merriest.	There was a good benefit and the farmer was merry.
Voru þeir þar um nóttina.	Were they there about the-night.	They were there that night.
Um morguninn er þeir Bolli voru ferðar búnir þá mælti Óttar:	About morning when they Bolli were travel preparing then spoke Ottar.	In the morning, when Bolli and his men were ready to go, Ottar said:
"Vel hefir þú gert Bolli er þú hefir sótt heim bæ minn.	"Well have you done Bolli that you have sought home farm mine.	"You have done well, Bolli, when you have visited my farm.
Vil eg og sýna þér lítið tillæti, gefa þér gullhring og kunna þökk að þú þiggir.	Wish I also show you little deference, give you gold-ring and know thanks that you accept.	I also want to show you a little favour, and give you a gold ring and I would be thankful if you accept.
Hér er og fingurgull er fylgja skal".	Here is also gold-ring that follow shall".	Here is also a gold ring to go with it".
Bolli þiggur gjafirnar og þakkar bónda.	Bolli accepted the-gifts and thanks the-farmer.	Bolli accepted the gifts and thanked the farmer.
Óttar var á hesti sínum því næst og reið fyrir þeim leiðina því að fallið hafði snjór lítill um nóttina.	Ottar was about horse his as nearest and rode ahead them the-way because that fallen had snow little about the-night.	Ottar was then on his horse, and rode in front of them, for little snow had fallen that night.
Þeir ríða nú veg sinn út til Svarfaðardals.	They rode now way theirs out to Svarfadardal.	They now rode their way out to Svarfadardal,
Og er þeir hafa eigi lengi riðið snerist hann við Óttar og mælti til Bolla:	And when they had not long ridden turned he with Ottar and spoke to Bolli.	and when they had not ridden long, Ottar turned to Bolli and said:
"Það mun eg sýna að eg vildi að þú værir vin minn.	"That should I show that I wish that you be friend mine.	"I will show that I wish you to be my friend.
Er hér annar gullhringur er eg vil þér gefa.	Is here another gold-ring that I wish to-you to-give.	Here's another gold ring I want to give you.
Væri eg yður vel viljaður í því er eg mætti.	Be I your well-willing willing for accordingly as I might.	I wish to help you in any way that I might.
Munuð þér og þess þurfa".	Shall you also this need".	If you shall need it".

The Tale of Bolli Bollason (Old Icelandic)

Old Icelandic	Literal	English
Bolli kvað bónda fara stórmannlega til sín "en þó vil eg þiggja hringinn".	Bolli thanked the-farmer going great-man-ness to him "but though wish I to-accept the-ring".	Bolli thanked the farmer for being so generous, "but still I want to accept the ring".
"Þá gerir þú vel", segir bóndi.	"Then doing you well", said the-farmer.	"Then you do well", said the farmer.

9

Nú er að segja frá Þorsteini af Hálsi.	Now is to say from Thorstein of Hals.	Now the story turns to Thorstein of Hals.
Þegar honum þykir von að Bolli muni norðan ríða þá safnar hann mönnum og ætlar að sitja fyrir Bolla og vill nú að verði umskipti um mál þeirra Helga.	When he thought expected that Bolli would north ride then collected he men and intended to sit-in-ambush before Bolli and wishing now to become about-exchanged about the-matter theirs Helgi.	When he expected Bolli to ride north, he gathered men and intended to sit in ambush before Bolli, and now wished to alter the matter between him and Helgi.
Þeir Þorsteinn hafa þrjá tigi manna og ríða fram til Svarfaðardalsár og setjast þar.	They Thorstein had three ten men and rode from to Svarfadardal and stayed there.	Thorstein and his men had thirty men, and rode up to Svarfadardal, and settled there.
Ljótur hét maður er bjó á Völlum í Svarfaðardal.	Ljot was-named a-man who lived at Vellir in Svarfadardal.	There was a man named Ljot, who lived at Vellir in Svarfadardal.
Hann var höfðingi mikill og vinsæll og málamaður mikill.	He was chieftain great and popular and law-man great.	He was a great chieftain, popular, and a great man of law.
Það var búningur hans hversdaglega að hann hafði svartan kyrtil og refði í hendi en ef hann bjóst til víga þá hafði hann blán kyrtil og öxi snaghyrnda.	It was costume his everyday that he had a-black tunic and poleaxe in hand but if he prepared to fight then had he a-blue tunic and axe snag-cornered.	It was his everyday costume that he had a black tunic and a poleaxe in his hand, but if he was preparing for battle, he had a blue tunic and a sharp-edged axe.
Var hann þá heldur ófrýnlegur.	Was he then rather inconspicuous.	He was then rather inconspicuous.
Þeir Bolli ríða út eftir Svarfaðardal.	They Bolli rode out along Svarfadardal.	Bolli and his men rode out along Svarfadardal.
Fylgir Óttar þeim út um bæinn að Hálsi og að ánni út.	Followed Ottar them out about the-farm at Hals and to-the-river from.	Ottar followed them out of the town at Hals and out to the river.

The Tale of Bolli Bollason (Old Icelandic)

Old Icelandic	Literal	English
Þar sat fyrir þeim Þorsteinn við sína menn og þegar er Óttar sér fyrirsátina bregður hann við og keyrir hest sinn þvers í brott.	There sat before them Thorstein with his men and when that Ottar saw for-the-ambush broke he with and spurred horse his across to away.	There Thorstein sat before them with his men, and when Ottar saw the ambush, he responded and drove his horse across.
Þeir Bolli ríða að djarflega og er þeir Þorsteinn sjá það og hans menn spretta þeir upp.	They Bolli rode to boldly and when they Thorstein saw that and his men sprang they up.	Bolli and his men rode boldly, and when Thorstein and his men saw it, they sprang up.
Þeir voru sínum megin ár hvorir en áin var leyst með löndum en ís flaut á miðri.	There were they sides the-river opposite about the-river was down with land was ice floating in the-middle.	They were on either side of the river, but the river flowed with land, and ice floated in the middle.
Hleypa þeir Þorsteinn út á ísinn.	Ran they Thorstein out into the-ice.	Thorstein and his men ran out onto the ice.
Helgi af Skeiði var og þar og eggjar þá fast og kvað nú vel að þeir Bolli reyndu hvort honum væri kapp sitt og metnaður einhlítt eða hvort nokkurir menn norður þar mundu þora að halda til móts við hann.	Helgi of Skeid was also there and encouraged then closely and said now well that they Bolli test whether he was eager his and pride unanimously or whether some men north there would dare to hold to meet with him.	Helgi of Skeid was also there and encouraged them, and said that Bolli and his men would be tested as to whether he was eagerness and pride would be unanimous, or whether there were men of the north who would dare to meet him.
"Þarf nú og eigi að spara að drepa þá alla.	"Need now and not that spare to kill then all.	"We do not need to spare from killing them all.
Mun það og leiða öðrum", sagði Helgi, "að veita oss ágang".	Would it also loath others", said Helgi, "that giving us aggression".	As it would also deter others", said Helgi, "from attacking us".
Bolli heyrir orð Helga og sér hvar hann er kominn út á ísinn.	Bolli heard words Helgi's and saw where he had come out on the-ice.	Bolli heard Helgi's words and saw where he had come out on the ice.
Bolli skýtur að honum spjóti og kemur á hann miðjan.	Bolli shot at him spear and came it his middle.	Bolli shot at him with a spear, and struck him in the middle.
Fellur hann á bak aftur í ána en spjótið flýgur í bakkann öðrum megum svo að fast var og hékk Helgi þar á niður í ána.	Fell he on back back in river but the-spear followed the bank other may so that fastened was and hung Helgi there at down in the-river.	He fell backwards into the river, but the spear flew into the bank the other way, so that it was stuck, and Helgi hung down there in the river.

The Tale of Bolli Bollason (Old Icelandic)

Old Icelandic	Literal	English
Eftir það tókst þar bardagi hinn skarpasti.	After that took there battle the hardest.	After that, the battle became the hardest.
Bolli gengur að svo fast að þeir hrökkva undan er nær voru.	Bolli went to so fast that they recoiled away-from who near were.	Bolli went so fast that those who were near him recoiled.
Þá sótti fram Þorsteinn í móti Bolla og þegar þeir fundust höggur Bolli til Þorsteins á öxlina og varð það mikið sár.	Then sought from Thorstein to meet Bolli and then they found striking Bolli to Thorstein's with an-axe and became that much wounding.	Then Thorstein went out to meet Bolli, and when they met, Bolli struck Thorstein on the shoulder, and it was a great wound.
Annað sár fékk Þorsteinn á fæti.	Another wound got Thorstein about the-leg.	Thorstein received another wound on his leg.
Sóknin var hin harðasta.	The-struggle was the hardest.	The attack was the hardest.
Bolli varð og sár nokkuð og þó ekki mjög.	Bolli became also wounded somewhat and though not much.	Bolli was also slightly injured, but not very badly.
Nú er að segja frá Óttari.	Now is to say from Ottar.	Now the story turns to Ottar.
Hann ríður upp á Völlu til Ljóts og þegar þeir finnast mælti Óttar:	He rode up to Vellir to Ljot and then they met spoke Ottar.	He rode up to Vellir, to Ljot, and when they met Ottar spoke:
"Eigi er nú setuefni Ljótur", sagði hann, "og fylg þú nú virðing þinni er þér liggur laus fyrir".	"Not is now sitting Ljot", said he, "and follows you now honour yours that you lay less for".	"No cause to sit about, Ljot", he said, "what follows now is your honour to prove".
"Hvað er nú helst í því Óttar?"	"What is now rather that according Ottar?"	"What would that involve, Ottar?"
"Eg hygg að þeir berjist hér niðri við ána Þorsteinn af Hálsi og Bolli og er það hin mesta hamingja að skirra vandræðum þeirra".	"I think that they fight here down by the-river Thorstein of Hals and Bolli and is that the most fortunate that prevent trouble theirs".	"I expect that they will be fighting here down by the river, Thorstein of Hals and Bolli, and it would be most fortunate to prevent their hostilities".
Ljótur mælti:	Ljot spoke.	Ljot spoke:
"Oft sýnir þú af þér mikinn drengskap".	"Often showed you of your great honour".	"You have often showed great honour".

The Tale of Bolli Bollason (Old Icelandic)

Old Icelandic	Literal	English
Ljótur brá við skjótt og við nokkura menn og þeir Óttar báðir.	Ljot startled with quickly and with several men and they Ottar both.	He reacted quickly and with several others hurried back to Ottar.
Og er þeir koma til árinnar berjast þeir Bolli sem óðast.	And when they came to the-river fought they Bolli as furious.	And when they came to the river, Bolli and the others were fighting furiously.
Voru þá fallnir þrír menn af Þorsteini.	Were they fallen three men of Thorstein's.	There were three of Thorstein's men that had fallen.
Þeir Ljótur ganga fram í meðal þeirra snarlega svo að þeir máttu nær ekki að hafast.	Then Ljot went from to between them quickly so that they may close not to have.	Ljot and his men quickly ran between the fighters so that they could not get close.
Þá mælti Ljótur:	Then spoke Ljot.	Then Ljot spoke:
"Þér skuluð skilja þegar í stað", segir hann, "og er þó nú ærið að orðið.	"You should separate immediately this place", said he, "and is though now plenty-of has become.	"You should separate immediately from this place", he said, "and now more than enough has been done.
Vil eg einn gera milli yðvar um þessi mál en ef því níta aðrir hvorir þá skulum vér veita þeim atgöngu".	Wish I alone to-do between you about this matter that if therefore refuse others each then should we grant them to-going".	I alone wish to decide to settle this matter, and if either of you refuses, then they shall be granted an attack".
En með því að Ljótur gekk að svo fast þá hættu þeir að berjast og því játtu hvorirtveggju að Ljótur skyldi gera um þetta þeirra í milli.	Then with because that Ljot went that so close then stop they the fight and therefore agreed either-side that Ljot should do about that their in between.	Then because Ljot went so close, they stopped fighting, and either side agreed, that Ljot should handle the matter between them.
Skildust þeir við svo búið.	Separated they with so prepared.	They parted ways so prepared.
Fór Þorsteinn heim en Ljótur býður þeim Bolla heim með sér og það þiggur hann.	Went Thorstein home and Ljot invited them Bolli home with him and that accepted he.	Thorstein went home, but Ljot invited Bolli and his men home with him, and he accepted.
Fóru þeir Bolli á Völlu til Ljóts.	Went they Bolli to Vellir to Ljot's.	Bolli and his men went to Vellir to Ljot's.
Þar heitir í Hestanesi sem þeir höfðu barist.	There named is Hestanes which they had bears.	There is named Hestanes, which bears today.

The Tale of Bolli Bollason (Old Icelandic)

Old Icelandic	Literal	English
Óttar bóndi skildist eigi fyrri við þá Bolla en þeir komu heim með Ljóti.	Ottar the-farmer separated not before with then Bolli then they came home with Ljot.	Farmer Ottar did not part with Bolli until they came home with Ljot.
Gaf Bolli honum stórmannlegar gjafar að skilnaði og þakkaði honum vel sitt liðsinni.	Gave Bolli him great-man-like gifts as parted and thanked him well this assistance.	Bolli gave him great gifts at parting, and thanked him well for his help.
Hét Bolli Óttari sinni vináttu.	Pledged Bolli Ottar his friendship.	Bolli pledged Ottar his friendship.
Fór hann heim til Krossa og sat í búi sínu.	Travelled he home to Krossar and stayed in farm his.	He went home to Krossar and stayed at his farm.

10

Eftir bardagann í Hestanesi fór Bolli heim með Ljóti á Völlu við alla sína menn en Ljótur bindur sár þeirra og greru þau skjótt því að gaumur var að gefinn.	After the-battle at Hestanes travelled Bolli home with Ljot to Vellir with all his men then Ljot bound wounds theirs and healed they quickly because that attention were for given.	After the battle in Hestanes, Bolli went home with Ljot at Vellir with all his men, where Ljot bound up their wounds, and they healed quickly, for the attention was paid to them.
En er þeir voru heilir sára sinna þá stefndi Ljótur þing fjölmennt.	Then when they were safe wounds theirs then summoned Ljot assembly full-of-people.	Then when they were healed of their wounds, Ljot convened a great assembly.
Riðu þeir Bolli á þingið.	Rode they Bolli to the-assembly.	Bolli and his men rode to the assembly.
Þar kom og Þorsteinn af Hálsi við sína menn.	There came also Thorstein of Hals with his men.	Thorstein of Hals also came there with his men.
Og er þingið var sett mælti Ljótur:	And when the-assembly was set spoke Ljot.	And when the Thing was set, Ljot said,
"Nú skal ekki fresta uppsögn um gerð þá er eg hefi samið milli þeirra Þorsteins af Hálsi og Bolla.	"Now shall not postpone up-saying about made then but I have agreement between they Thorstein's of Hals and Bolli.	"Now the conclusion of the agreement which I have brought up between Thorstein of Hals and Bolli shall not be postponed.
Hefi eg það upphaf að gerðinni að Helgi skal hafa fallið óheilagur fyrir illyrði sín og tiltekju við Bolla.	Have I that begun to make that Helgi shall have failed unholy for ill-words his and exchange with Bolli.	I have the beginning of the deed, that Helgi has fallen without right for compensation for his wickedness and betrayal of Bolli.

The Tale of Bolli Bollason (Old Icelandic)

Old Icelandic	Literal	English
Sárum þeirra Þorsteins og Bolla jafna eg saman.	The-wounds they Thorstein's and Bolli equal I the-same.	I will make amends for the wounds of Thorstein and Bolli,
En þá þrjá menn er féllu af Þorsteini skal Bolli bæta.	But they three men who fell of Thorstein shall Bolli compensate.	but the three men who fell from Thorstein shall be compensated by Bolli.
En fyrir fjörráð við Bolla og fyrirsát skal Þorsteinn greiða honum fimmtán hundruð þriggja alna aura.	But for plotting-against with Bolli and ambush shall Thorstein assist him fifteen hundred three ells pay.	But for the conspiracy and plotting-against Bolli, Thorstein shall pay him fifteen hundred three cubit lengths of homespun cloth.
Skulu þeir að þessu alsáttir".	Shall they at this all-settle".	They shall all settle at this".
Eftir þetta var slitið þinginu.	After it was dissolved the-assembly.	After that the assembly was dissolved.
Segir Bolli Ljóti að hann mun ríða heimleiðis og þakkar honum vel alla sína liðveislu og skiptust þeir fögrum gjöfum við og skildu við góðum vinskap.	Told Bolli Ljot that he would ride home-ways and thanked him well all his assistance and exchanged they fair gifts with and separated with good friendship.	Bolli told Ljot that he would ride home, and thanked him well for all his help, and they exchanged beautiful gifts and parted with good friendship.
Bolli tók upp bú Sigríðar á Skeiði því að hún vildi fara vestur með honum.	Bolli took up the-farm Sigrid of Skeid because that she wished to-travel west with him.	Bolli took up Sigrid's estate at Skeid, because she wanted to go west with him.
Ríða þau veg sinn þar til er þau koma á Miklabæ til Arnórs.	Rode they way theirs there until that they came to Miklabaer to Arnor's.	They rode their way, until they came to Miklabær to Arnor.
Tók hann harðla vel við þeim.	Took he greatly well with them.	He received them very kindly,
Dvöldust þar um hríð og sagði Bolli Arnóri allt um skipti þeirra Svarfdæla hversu farið hafði.	Dwelled there about awhile and told Bolli Arnor all about exchanged theirs Svarfadardal how-so gone had.	they stayed there for a while, and Bolli told Arnor all about the exchange of the Svarfadardal, and how things had gone.
Arnór mælti:	Arnor spoke.	Arnor said:
"Mikla heill hefir þú til borið um ferð þessa við slíkan mann sem þú áttir þar er Þorsteinn var.	"Much luck have you to bear about journey this with such a-man as you have there as Thorstein was.	"You have been very lucky in this journey, and in your dealings with such a man as Thorstein.

The Tale of Bolli Bollason (Old Icelandic)

Old Icelandic	Literal	English
Er það sannast um að tala að fáir eða öngvir höfðingjar munu sótt hafa meira frama úr öðrum héruðum norður hingað en þú, þeir sem jafnmarga öfundarmenn áttu hér fyrir".	Is it true about that said that few or none chieftains should attend have more honour of other provinces north here than you, they who equal-many slanderous-men had here for".	Is it true to say that few or no chiefs will have sought more fame from other provinces north here than you, those who had so many envious people here before".
Bolli ríður nú í brott af Miklabæ við sína menn og heim suður.	Bolli rode now to away from Miklabaer with his men and home south.	Bolli now rode away from Miklabær with his men and home south.
Tala þeir Arnór til vináttu með sér af nýju að skilnaði.	Spoke they Arnor to friendship with them of anew at parting.	Bolli and Arnor spoke of friendship anew before parting.
En er Bolli kom heim í Tungu varð Þórdís húsfreyja hans honum fegin.	Then when Bolli came home to Tunga was Thordis housewife his to-him relieved.	But when Bolli came home to Tunga, Thordis, his housewife, was glad to see him.
Hafði hún frétt áður nokkuð af róstum þeirra Norðlendinga og þótti mikið í hættu að honum tækist vel til.	Had she news before some of unruliness theirs The-northerners and thought much at danger that he took well to.	She had heard something before about the skirmishes of the Northerners, and thought it was very dangerous for him to succeed.
Situr Bolli nú í búi sínu með mikilli virðingu.	Stayed Bolli now at farm his with much honour.	Bolli now stayed in his estate with great honour.
Þessi ferð Bolla var ger að nýjum sögum um allar sveitir og töluðu allir einn veg um að slík þótti varla farin hafa verið nálega.	This journey Bolli's was made to new sagas about all areas and told all one way about that such thought barely gone had been near-to.	This journey of Bolli was the subject of new stories about all the districts, and everyone agreed that such a thing was scarcely thought to have been equalled.
Óx virðing hans af slíku og mörgu öðru.	Grew respect his of such and many others.	His respect from this and many other things grew.
Bolli fékk Sigríði gjaforð göfugt og lauk vel við hana.	Bolli found Sigrid married worthy and concluded well with her.	Bolli gave Sigrid a noble marriage match and it concluded well,
Og höfum vér eigi heyrt þessa sögu lengri.	And have we none heard this saga longer.	and we have not heard any more of this story.

Word List *(Old Icelandic to English)*

Old Icelandic	English

A, a

að	a, about, as, at, for, from, has, have, in, it, of, that, the, to
aðra	another
aðrir	others
af	at, from, from, of, of, off, to
afglapa	foolish
afréttum	the-pastures
aftur	back, down, return, returned
albúnir	all-prepared
aldrei	never
aldri	age
alist	homes
alla	all, all
allan	all
allar	all
allir	all, all
allra	of-all
allri	all
alls	all
allstórmannlega	all-great-man-like
allt	all, all
allvel	all-well, all-well
alna	ells
alsáttir	all-settle
alþingi	the-assembly
andvirki	haystacks
annað	another, another, other
annar	another, another
annarri	another
Arnór	Arnor (name)
Arnóri	Arnor (name)
Arnórs	Arnor's (name)
atgöngu	to-going
atkvæðum	charges
auðigur	rich
aura	pay

Á, á

Á	about, as, at, for, from, in, into, it, of, on, the, to, up, was, with
áðu	to
áður	before, earlier
ágætir	renowned
ágætlega	greatly
ágang	aggression
áin	the-river
ána	river, the-river, the-river
ánni	the-river
ár	the-river
árinnar	the-river
ásjá	assistance, assistance
ásjár	assistance
áskoran	challenge
ást	to
átján	eighteen, eighteen
átt	had
átta	eight
átti	had, married
áttir	have
áttu	had, have-you

Æ, æ

æðimaður	frenzy-man
æja	rest
ærið	plenty-of
ærin	considerable
ætla	expect, intend, intended
ætlað	intended, plans
ætlar	intend, intended
ættsmár	of-family-small

Word List (Old Icelandic to English)

Old Icelandic	English

B, b

Old Icelandic	English
bað	asked, ordered
báðir	both
bæ	a-farm, farm
bæinn	the-farm
bænum	farmhouse, the-farm
bæta	better, compensate
bak	back
baki	horseback
bakkann	bank
bardagann	the-battle
bardagi	battle
barist	bears
Barst	overcome
bauð	invited
beiða	offer
beiðast	ask
beiddi	asked
beini	benefit
belti	belt
ber	bear
berjast	fight, fought
berjist	fight
best	best
besta	best
bestur	best
betra	better
betri	better
betur	better
biðja	offer
bíður	wait
bindur	bound
Bjarnar	Bjarni (name)
bjó	lived
bjóða	offer, to-invite
bjóst	prepared
bjuggu	lived
blán	a-blue
blárri	black
blíðu	joyfulness
blika	shining
boðið	bid, offered
boli	the-bull

Old Icelandic	English
Bolla	Bolli (name), Bolli's (name)
Bollason	Bollason (name), Son-of-Bolli (name)
Bollasyni	Bollason (name)
Bolli	Bolli (name)
bónda	husband, the-farmer
bóndi	farmer, host, the-farmer
borið	bear, carried
börnum	children
brá	startled
bræðra	the-brothers
bræður	brothers
braut	broke
bregða	break
bregður	broke, drew
brekráð	treachery
bróðir	brother
bróður	brother
brosti	laughed
brotið	broken
brott	away
bú	the-farm
búa	settlers
búast	prepare
búðardyrunum	the-booth-doors
búðina	the-booth
búi	farm
búið	prepared
búin	prepared
bundinn	bound
búningur	costume
búnir	preparing
býður	invited
býr	prepared
býst	prepared

D, d

Old Icelandic	English
dauður	dead
desjarnar	the-hay
djarflega	boldly
Dögurðarnes	Dagverdarnes (place)
dóm	self-judgement

Word List (Old Icelandic to English)

Old Icelandic	English
dregur	drew
drengilegsta	bravely
drengskap	honour
drepa	kill
drepið	kill, killing
Dvöldust	dwelled
dýrsta	dearest

E, e

Old Icelandic	English
eða	an, and, or
ef	if
efni	matter, the-matter
efnilegastur	promising
eftir	after, afterwards, along
eftirmálinu	the-after-matter
eftirmáls	after-matter
eg	I
eggjar	encouraged
eiga	have, in, to-have
eigi	no, none, not
eign	own
eigna	own
eina	one
einhlítt	unanimously
einir	only
einn	alone, one, only
einnhvern	one
einsætt	one-agreement
einum	any
ekki	no, not, nothing
en	about, and, but, in, nor, since, than, that, then, was, what, whether
enga	none
engi	no, none
engis	none
engrar	no, none
engu	nothing
enn	but, the, then
er	am, and, are, as, but, had, is, it-is, that, the, then, was, were, when, which, who
erfið	difficulty
ert	have
ertu	are-you
eru	are, are-there, is, there, were
eruð	are
eyða	devastate

F, f

Old Icelandic	English
fá	fee, got
Fær	accomplished, got, travelled
færa	bring, bringing
færi	travel, way-out
fæti	the-leg
fagnað	welcomed
fagnaði	celebration
fáir	few
fálega	coldly, poorly
fallið	failed, fallen, make
fallnir	fallen
fangi	arms
fann	found
fár	few
fara	go, going, to-travel, travel
faraskjóta	horses
farið	fared, gone, travel, travelled
farin	gone
farinn	travelling
fast	close, closely, fast, fastened
fátt	few
fé	cattle, fee, wealth
fébótum	compensation
fegin	relieved
fékk	found, got
félagar	comrades
félagsskap	comradeship
felldur	falling
féllu	well
fellur	fell
fengi	gets

Word List (Old Icelandic to English)

Old Icelandic	English
fer	goes, set-out, travelled, travels
ferð	going, journey, travel, travelling
ferðar	travel
ferðina	going
ferðinni	the-journey, travel
ferðir	journey
fimmtán	fifteen
fingurgull	gold-ring
finna	find
finnast	encounter, met
finnum	find
fjandskap	fiendship
fjár	of-wealth, wealth
fjarri	far-away
fjölmenna	following-men, many-men
fjölmenni	followers-many
fjölmennt	full-of-people
fjórðungi	district
fjörráð	plotting, plotting-against
fláráðum	treacherous
flaut	floating
fleiri	more
flokk	flock
flýgur	followed
flytjir	with-fleetness
fögrum	fair
fólið	foolishly
fólsku	false, falsehood
fór	did, goes, travelled, went
fórstu	travelled-you
Fóru	travelled, went
förum	a-journey
förunautar	companions, companions
Fótbít	Leg-Biter (name)
frá	from
frægðarverk	famous-work
frænda	kinsman
frændkona	kinswoman
frændkonu	kinswoman
fram	from
frama	honour, honour
framar	honour
freista	test, try
fresta	postpone
frétt	news
frétti	asking, learned
Fréttist	reported
Fréttust	reported
fríð	peaceful
fritt	safe
fund	meet
fundur	a-meeting
fundust	found, met
fylg	follows
fylgi	follows
Fylgir	followed
fylgja	follow
fylgt	followed
fyrir	ahead, because-of, before, for
fyrirsát	ambush
fyrirsátina	for-the-ambush
fyrr	before
fyrri	before
fyrrum	before-us

G, g

Old Icelandic	English
gaf	gave
gáfu	gave
Galmarströnd	Galmarstrond (place)
ganga	go, went
gangi	going
gaumur	attention
gefa	give, to-give
gefið	give
gefinn	given
gegnir	serves
gegnum	through
gekk	went
Gengið	gone
gengu	went
gengur	came, went
ger	made
gera	do, doing, to-do
gerð	made

Word List (Old Icelandic to English)

Old Icelandic	English
gerði	did, made
gerðinni	make
gerðu	did, made
gerið	do
gerir	do, doing
gert	done, made
getið	got
getur	got
giftuvænlegur	luck-promised
gjafar	gifts
gjafir	gifts, the-gift
gjafirnar	the-gifts
gjaforð	married
gjalda	pay
gjöfum	gifts
glaðasti	gladdest
gnótt	an-abundance
góða	good
góðar	good
góðum	good
góður	good
göfgustu	noblest
göfugt	worthy
gott	benefit
graðung	bull
Graðungur	bull
graðungurinn	the-bull
grán	grey
greiða	assist
greiddist	resolved
greru	healed
griðung	a-bull
grípa	grab
gripirnir	treasures
grjóti	rocks
grunaði	suspected
grunur	suspect
Guðdala-Starra	Starri-of-Guddalir
Guðdölum	Guddalir (place)
Guðmundar	Gudmund (name)
Guðmundur	Gudmund (name)
Guðrún	Gudrun (name)
gullhring	gold-ring
gullhringinn	gold-ring
gullhringur	gold-ring

Old Icelandic	English
gulllagðan	gold-laid
gullrekna	gold-inlaid
gyrður	buckled

H, h

hæðileg	mockery
hæglegt	easily
hægt	possible
hættu	danger, stop
Haf	have
hafa	had, have, to-have
hafast	have
hafði	had, has
hafi	had
Hafið	have
hafir	have
haft	had, have
haga	fairly
halda	hold
haldinn	holds
hálfan	half
hálfs	half-month's
hallaði	turned
Háls	Hals (place)
Hálsi	Hals (place)
hamingja	fortunate, luck
hana	he, her
hann	cowardly, he, him, his
hans	him, his
harðasta	hardest
harðla	greatly
harmaði	mourned
héðan	from-here
héðra	district
hefði	has
Hefi	have
hefir	had, has, have
hefur	had
Hegranessþingi	Hegranes (place)-Assembly
Hegranessþings	Hegranes (place)-Assembly
heiðina	the-heath
heilir	safe

Word List (Old Icelandic to English)

Old Icelandic	English
heill	luck
heim	home
heima	home
heiman	at-home, from-home
heimanferð	from-home-travel
heimboðanna	home-invitation
heimboðum	home-invitations
heimleiðis	home-ways
heimsklega	foolishly
heimsklegast	foolishly
heimskur	foolishness
heimsótt	home-sought
heimti	asked-for
heimul	have-right
heitaðist	called
heiti	am-named
heitinn	named
heitir	named
hékk	hung
heldur	behind, rather
Helga	Helgi (name), Helgi's (name)
Helgi	Helgi (name)
Heljardalsheiði	Heljardal Heath (place)
Hellu-Narfa	Hellu-Narfi (name)
Hellu-Narfasonar	Hellu-Narfason (name)
helst	rather
hélt	held
hendi	hand
hendur	hand
hennar	hers
henni	her
hér	here
héraði	district
héruð	district
héruðum	provinces
hest	horse
hesta	horses
hestana	horses, the-horses
Hestanesi	Hestanes (place)
hesti	horse
hestsins	horse's
hét	named, pledged, promised, was-named
hey	hay, hey
heygarð	hay-stacks
heygjöfinni	hay-giving
heyinu	the-hay
heyjum	hay
heyrði	heard
heyrir	heard
heyrt	heard
heyvöndul	a-haystack, hay-bundle
hið	the
hin	the
Hina	the, these
hingað	here
hinn	the
hins	the
hinu	the
hinum	the
Hitt	find
hitti	met
hittust	met
hjá	beside
hjálm	helmet
Hjaltadal	Hjaltadal (place)
Hjaltasona	Hjaltasons (name)
Hjaltasonu	Hjaltasons (name)
Hjaltasynir	Hjaltasons (name), Sons-of-Hjalti (name)
Hjarðarholti	Hjardarholt (place)
hlaupi	running
Hleypa	ran
hleypur	ran
hlið	side
hlíðinni	the-slope
hljóp	leapt, ran
hljópu	ran
hljótum	we-get
hlut	lot
hlutir	things
hníf	knife
hóf	began
Höfða	Hofdi (place)
höfðingi	chieftain

Word List (Old Icelandic to English)

Old Icelandic	English
höfðingjar	chieftains
höfðu	had
Hofi	Hof (place)
Hofs	Hof (place)
höfuð	head
Höfum	has, have
höggur	striking
holinu	hollow
hönd	hand
höndum	hand, his-hands
honum	he, him, his, to-him
horfa	turn
horfist	looks
horn	horn
hót	threat
hríð	awhile
hringinn	the-ring
hrökkva	recoiled
hrossin	herd
Hrútafirði	Hrutafjord (place)
Hrútafjarðar	Hrutafjord (place)
húðfat	bed-roll
hugði	think
hugðu	thought
hugðum	think
hugsar	thought
hún	she
hundruð	hundred
hús	a-house
húsfreyja	housewife
húsfreyju	housewife
hvað	what
hvar	what, where
hvarf	broke-away
hver	who
hverfa	turn
hverfið	turn
hvergi	neither
Hverja	what
Hverjir	who
hverju	every
hvern	what
hversdaglega	everyday
hversu	how, how-so
hvert	each, how, what, which
hvítur	white
hvolfinu	half
hvorir	each, opposite
hvorirtveggju	either-side
hvort	how, whether
hygg	think
hyggja	think

I, i

ill	ill
illa	bad, ill
illmæli	slander
illt	bad-terms, ill
illu	evil
illyrði	ill-words
inn	inside
innan	inside

Í, í

í	about, at, for, in, into, is, it, on, that, the, this, to
íhlutunarsamur	in-sharing-together
ís	ice
ísinn	the-ice

J, j

jafna	equal
jafnan	usually
jafnmarga	equal-many
jafnsaman	together
jarðhús	earth-house
járna	iron-shod
játtu	agreed
jól	Yule (name)
jörð	earth, the-earth

Word List (Old Icelandic to English)

Old Icelandic	English	Old Icelandic	English
K, k		**L, l**	
kærleikum	friendship	lætur	had
kalla	declare	lagði	became, lunged
kallaður	called	lagður	laid
kapp	eager	lagt	had
kappi	warriors	láta	allow, leave
kápu	cape	látum	let
kasta	cast	laug	bathe
kátasti	merriest	lauk	concluded
kaupmenn	trading-men	launmaðurinn	the-unseen-man
kaupmönnum	trading-men	laus	less
kemur	came, come, coming	leggið	lay
kerlingarnef	Crone's-Nose (name)	leggja	have, lay
keyrði	spurred	leggur	lunged
keyrir	spurred	leið	journey, passed, way
klæði	clothing	leiða	loath
klaufir	hooves	leiðina	the-way
Kom	came, come	leiðréttu	rectify
koma	came, coming	leik	game
komið	came, come	leika	sport
kominn	came, come	leikum	sport
komir	come	leit	saw
komnir	come, coming	leita	look, seek
komu	came	leitast	seek
komum	come	lengi	long
kona	wife, wife-of	lengri	longer
konu	wife	lengur	any-longer
konungsnaut	king's-gift	lést	said
kostur	chose	lét	had, let
Krossa	Krossar (place)	léti	let
Krossum	Krossar (place)	Letja	discourage
kunna	know	letjast	dissuaded
kvað	said, spoke, thanked	létti	relieved
kvaddi	greeted	léttu	relieved
kveddi	greeting	létu	led, let
kveldið	evening	leyst	down, solved
kvisti	trim	leystur	releasing
kyrrt	peace, still	liðfærri	company-less
kyrtil	tunic	liðsafla	company-provided
kýstu	choosing	liðsinnaður	team-minded
		liðsinni	assistance
		líður	passed
		liðveislu	assistance
		liggur	lay

112

Word List (Old Icelandic to English)

Old Icelandic	English
líst	appears
líta	look
lítið	little
lítill	little
lítils	little
lítinn	a-little
litlu	little
litu	looked
Ljóti	Ljot (name), Ljot (place)
Ljóts	Ljot (place), Ljot's (name)
Ljótur	Ljot (name)
lögum	law
lokið	finished
löndum	land
lýsa	describe, show
lýst	shown

M, m

Old Icelandic	English
má	may
maður	a-man, man
maðurinn	the-man
mælt	talked
mælti	speaking, spoke
mæltu	spoke
mæta	meet
mætti	may, might
mágsemd	in-laws
mágsemdar	as-in-laws
maklegt	deserve
mál	case, matter, speak-to, the-matter
málamaður	law-man, man-of-law
máli	discuss, matter, speak, the-matter
málið	the-case, the-matter
málinu	the-case
málóði	of-violent-language
málum	the-matter
mánaðar	a-month's
mann	a-man, men
manna	men, people's
mannfóli	an-idiot
manni	a-man, man
manninn	person
mannsins	the-man
mánuð	a-month
Marbæli	Marbaeli (place)
Marbælinga	Marbaeli (place)
marga	many
margt	many, much
marki	a-sign
máttu	may
með	with
meðal	between
mega	may
megi	may
megin	sides
megum	may
Meiddi	wounded
mein	harm
meir	more
meira	more
meiri	the-more
menn	men, people
mér	for-me, I, me, mine, to-me
merkur	marks
mest	most
mesta	most
mestum	most
metast	meet
metnaður	pride
miðjan	middle
miðri	the-middle
mig	me, mine, much, my
mikið	much
mikill	great, much
mikilli	much
mikinn	great, much
mikla	much
Miklabæ	Miklabaer (place)
miklir	great
miklu	much
miklum	much
milli	between
mín	mine, my
mína	mine, my
minn	mine

113

Word List (Old Icelandic to English)

Old Icelandic	English
minna	mine
minni	diminish, less
mínum	mine, my
mitt	mine
Mjög	great, many, much
Möðruvöllu	Modruvellir (place)
mönnum	men, people, to-people
mörgu	many
morguninn	morning
mót	meeting
móti	meet, return
móts	meet
Mun	shall, should, would
mund	about-that-time
mundi	should, would
mundu	would
muni	should, would
munt	should
muntu	shall-you, should-you
munu	shall, should, would, would-be
Munuð	shall
munum	shall, should

N, n

Old Icelandic	English
ná	obtain
nær	close, near, when
næst	nearest
nætur	nights
nafn	name, name
nálega	near-to
Narfason	Narfason (name)
náskyld	closely-related
nauðsyn	necessity
nauðsynja	deed-refuse
neins	any
nenni	care
níðingsverk	lowly-deed
niðri	down
niður	down, kinsman
níta	refuse
nokkuð	some, something, somewhat
nokkur	somewhat
nokkura	any, several, somewhat
nokkurir	some
norðan	north
Norðlendinga	the-northerners
Norðlendingum	northerners
norður	north
nóttina	the-night
nú	now, so
nýju	anew
nýjum	new

O, o

Old Icelandic	English
ofan	down
ofríki	rampages, un-rule, unruly
ofstýri	unmanageable
Oft	often
og	also, and
okkars	our
okkur	us
orð	words
orða	words
orði	word
orðið	become, words
orðinn	become
oss	ours, us

Ó, ó

Old Icelandic	English
óðafári	a-hurry
óðast	furious
ófæru	impassable
ófallið	misguided
ófarin	un-faring
ófrýnlegur	inconspicuous
óhæfu	unqualified
óheilagur	unholy
ójafnaðarmenn	un-equal-men
Ólafi	Olaf (name)
Ólafs	Olaf's (name)
Ólafur	Olaf (name)

Word List (Old Icelandic to English)

Old Icelandic	English
óliðdrjúgur	un-substantial-company
óliðlegt	unsuitable
ólman	wild
ómæt	un-good
ómannlegt	inhumane
óorðan	slanderous
óréttvís	un-right-knowing
Óttar	Ottar (name)
Óttari	Ottar (name)
óvinum	un-friends
óvinveittur	unfriendly
óvíst	uncertain
Óx	grew

Ö, ö

Old Icelandic	English
öðru	another, others
öðrum	another, other, others
öðruvís	other-knowing
öfundarmenn	slanderous-men
öll	all
öllu	all
öllum	all
ömbun	return
öngvir	none
öxi	axe
öxlina	an-axe

P, p

Old Icelandic	English
pá	Peacock (name)

R, r

Old Icelandic	English
ráð	advised, decide, declare
ráða	allow, decide
ráðast	arrange
ráðinn	riding
ráðlaus	ill-advised
ráðlegast	advice, advisable
ráðs	advice
ræddist	discussed
ræðst	rode
réði	decide
Réðst	rode
refði	poleaxe
reið	riding, rode
reifa	account-for
réttindum	right
réttvísi	right-knowing
Reykja	Reykir (place)
reyna	tested, trying
reyndu	test
ríð	ride
ríða	ride, rode, to-ride
riðið	ridden, ride
ríðið	ride
riðu	rode
ríður	rode
rífa	tearing
ríka	Powerful (name)
ríki	powerful
róstum	unruliness

S, s

Old Icelandic	English
Sá	saw, so
sækir	seek
sæmd	honour
sæmdar	honour
sæmdarauki	honour
sæmdir	honour
sæmdum	honour
sæta	sit-in-ambush
sætt	settle
sættast	reconcile
safnar	collected
sagði	said, said, told, told
sagt	said, told
sakir	conviction, for-the-sake-of, sake, the-charges
saman	the-same, together, together
samið	agreement
sannast	the-truest, true, truly

Word List (Old Icelandic to English)

Old Icelandic	English
sár	wound, wounded, wounding, wounds
sára	wounds
Sárum	the-wounds
Sat	sat, stayed
satt	TRUE
Sátu	sat, sitting, stayed
sáu	saw
sé	being, is, see, so, this, was
segi	say
segir	said, told
segja	say, to-say
seilast	obtain
sektan	outlawed
sekti	convicted
selja	repay
sem	as, as-if, that, which, who
sendi	send
sér	her, him, himself, his, saw, them, themselves
setið	stay
setjast	stayed
sett	set
settist	set
setuefni	sitting
Setur	set
séu	are, being
síðan	after, afterwards, then
síðar	afterwards
síðir	eventually
sig	him, himself, such
Sigríðar	Sigrid (name)
Sigríði	Sigrid (name)
Sigríður	Sigrid (name)
silfurs	of-silver
sín	him, his, this
sína	his, their, theirs
sinn	hers, his, theirs
sinna	his, theirs
sinni	his
síns	her, his
sínu	his
sínum	hers, his, theirs, they
sitja	sit, sit-in-ambush, sitting
sitt	his, this
Situr	stayed
sjá	saw
sjáandi	seeing
sjálfan	yourself
sjálfdæmi	self-judgement
sjö	seven
skaða	scathed
Skagafirði	Skagafjord (place)
Skagafjarðar	Skagafjord (place)
skal	shall, shall-be, should
skalt	shall
skaltu	shall, shall-you
skammt	a-short-distance, short-distance
skapi	mood
skapillur	bad-temper
skaplyndi	nature
skarpasti	hardest
Skeið	Skeid (place)
Skeiði	Skeid (place)
skelmi	devilish-man
skikkju	cloak
skildi	separated, shield
skildinum	the-shield
skildir	shields
skildist	separated
Skildu	separated
Skildust	separated
skilið	separated
skilja	separate, separated
skiljum	understanding
skilnaði	parted, parting
skinnstakki	skin-cloak
skip	a-ship
skips	ships
skipta	exchange
skipti	exchanged
skiptust	exchanged
skirra	prevent
skjöld	shield
Skjöldurinn	the-shield
skjótt	quickly
skógarmenn	forest-men

Word List (Old Icelandic to English)

Old Icelandic	English
skóggang	outlawry
skóggangssök	forest-seeking
sköllóttur	bald
skörulega	boldly
skörungur	noble
skuli	shall
Skulu	shall
skuluð	should
skulum	should
skyld	guilt
skyldi	should
skyldu	should
skýtur	shot
sleppa	escape
slík	such
slitið	dissolved
smærri	smaller
snaghyrnda	snag-cornered
snarlega	quickly
Sneri	turned
snerist	turned
snjór	snow
snúa	return, turn
sögu	saga
sögum	sagas
Sóknin	the-struggle
sökótt	accusations
sömu	same
Son	son, son-of
sonar	son
sonur	son, the-son-of
sótt	attend, attended, sought
sótti	sought
spara	spare
spekt	wisdom
spjót	spear
spjóti	spear
spjótið	spear, the-spear
spjótinu	spear
spretta	sprang
spyr	asked
stað	place
staddur	standing
stærimaður	Stately-man (name)
stærimann	Stately-man (name)
stærimanni	Stately-man (name)
standanda	stood
Starri	Starri (name)
stefna	agreement
stefndi	charged, summoned
stefnir	charged
stefnu	summoned, summons
stefnuna	the-summons
stefnunni	the-summons
stela	steal, stealing
stertimaður	Stately-man (name)
stíga	step
Stigu	dismounted
stóð	stood
stolið	stolen
stólkonungurinn	the-emperor
stórmannlega	great-man-ness
stórmannlegar	great-man-like
studdist	stood
stund	while
stýrimann	the-captain
styrk	strength
suður	south
sumar	summer
sumarið	summer
sundur	asunder
sundurþykki	discord
svarar	answered, said
Svarfaðardal	Svarfadardal (place)
Svarfaðardals	Svarfadardal (place)
Svarfaðardalsár	Svarfadardal (place)
Svarfdæla	Svarfadardal (place)
svarið	answer
svartan	a-black
sveininn	the-boy
sveinsins	son-yours
sveit	company
sveitir	areas
sveitum	the-district
sverðinu	the-sword
sviptir	loss
svo	so, 0
sýna	seemed, show
sýnir	showed
Sýnist	seemed

Word List (Old Icelandic to English)

Old Icelandic	English
sýnt	shown
systrungur	mother's-sister's-son

T, t

Old Icelandic	English
tæki	take
tækist	took
Tak	take
taka	take, taken
takir	take
tal	talking
tala	said, speak, spoke
talið	conversation
tauma	reins
tekið	taken
tekist	taken
tekur	took
tel	say
tíðinda	news
tigi	ten
til	about, its, to, until
tilfelli	occurrence
tillæti	deference
tiltekju	exchange
tíma	time
títt	reported
tók	took
tókst	took
tóku	took-to
tólf	twelve
töluðu	talked, told
torfstakka	turf-stacks
trausts	trust
Tungu	Tunga (place)
tvenn	twice
tvo	two

Þ, þ

Old Icelandic	English
Þá	the, then, they, when
það	is, it, so, that, this, to
þaðan	from-there
þætti	seems
Þakka	thanks
þakkaði	thanked
þakkar	thanked, thanks
þangað	from-there, there, there
þann	the, then
þar	here, it, there, there
Þarf	need
þarftu	need-you
Þau	they, they
þegar	as-soon-as, from-there, immediately, then, when
þeim	home, them, they, to-them
Þeir	the, then, there, they
þeirra	of-them, of-they, their, theirs, them, they, they-of
þenna	this
þér	to-you, you, your
þess	this
þessa	this
þessar	these
þessi	this
þessir	these
þessu	this
þetta	it, that, this
þið	you, you-two
þig	you
þiggir	accept
þiggja	accept, accepted, to-accept
þiggur	accepted
þína	yours
þing	assembly, the-assembly
þingið	the-assembly
þinginu	the-assembly
þingmaður	assembly-man
þingsins	the-assembly
þinn	you, yours
þinnar	yours
þinni	yours
þitt	yours
þjófarnir	thieves
þjófnað	theft

Word List (Old Icelandic to English)

Old Icelandic	English
þó	though
þökk	thanks
þola	endure
þora	dare
Þórð	Thord (name)
Þórðar	Thord (name)
Þórðarsonar	Son-of-Thord (name)
Þórði	Thord (name)
Þórdís	Thordis (name)
Þórður	Thord (name)
Þorgrímur	Thorgrim (name)
Þórólf	Thorolf (name)
Þórólfi	Thorolf (name)
Þórólfs	Thorolf's (name)
Þórólfur	Thorolf (name)
Þorstein	Thorstein (name), Thorstein (name)
Þorsteini	Thorstein (name), Thorstein's (name)
Þorsteinn	Thorstein (name)
Þorsteins	Thorstein's (name)
Þorvaldi	Thorvald (name), Thorvald (name)
Þorvaldur	Thorvald (name)
þótt	though
þótti	thought
þóttu	thought
þriggja	three
þrír	three
þrjá	three
þrjár	three
þú	you
Þúfum	Thufur (place)
þungt	negatively
þurfa	need
þurfi	need
Þverá	Thvera (place)
Þverár	Thvera (place)
þvers	across
því	according, accordingly, as, because, since, such, that, therefore
þykir	consider, seems, think, thought
þykist	think
þykjast	realised, think

U, u

Old Icelandic	English
um	about, with
umskipti	about-exchanged
undan	away-from
undir	into, near
undri	fool-of-yourself
ungur	young
upp	up, upped
upphaf	begun
uppi	up
uppsögn	up-saying
Urðskriðuhóla	Urdskriduholar (place)
urðu	became
utan	abroad

Ú, ú

Old Icelandic	English
úr	back-from, from, from-out-of, of, out-of
út	from, out
úti	outside

V, v

Old Icelandic	English
vænt	expect
Væri	be, was
værir	be, would-be
vanda	custom
vandi	difficulty
vandræði	dispute
vandræðum	trouble
Var	then, was, were
varð	became, was
varða	warranted
varði	expect
varðveislu	hospitality
varðveita	ward-knowing
varla	barely
varna	defence
varstu	where

Word List (Old Icelandic to English)

Old Icelandic	English
veður	weathered
veg	way
vegar	way
veisla	feast, the-feast
veislu	feast
Veit	know
veita	giving, grant
veitti	granted
vel	well, well-willing
velli	the-fields
venslum	marriage
Ver	be
vér	our, we
vera	be, becomes, being, be-it, were
verð	the-worth
verða	be, became, become, being, would-be
verðgang	vagrancy
verði	become
verðugt	worth
verður	becomes, worth
verið	been
verja	defend, guarding, protect
verk	work
versna	worse
verst	the-worst
vert	worthy
vesalmenni	wretch
vestur	west
vetra	winters
veturinn	winter
vexti	grown
við	against, by, to, with
viðtökur	with-taken, with-taking
víg	killing, slaying-of, the-killing-of, the-slaying-of
víga	fight
vígi	the-slaying
vígsmálið	fight-the-case
vil	will, wish
vildi	willing, wish, wished
vilja	will, willing, wish
viljaður	willing
vilji	wish
viljir	wish
Viljum	will
vill	wished, wishing
vilt	wish
vin	friend
vinátta	friendship
vináttu	friendship
vindur	the-wind
vinganarmál	friendship-matter
vingast	make-friends
vinhollir	open-whole
vinsæll	popular
vinskap	friendship
vinskapar	friendship
vinur	a-friend, friend
virða	value, worth
virðið	honour
virðing	honour, respect, worth, worthiness
virðingar	honour
virðingarvænlegt	respect-kindly
virðingu	honour
virkið	the-compound
víst	certainly
vistar	lodging
vísu	certainly
vita	know
vitja	visit
vitlaus	wit-less
voða	risk
Völlu	Vellir (place)
Völlum	Vellir (place)
von	expected, to-expect
vopn	weapons
vopnaðir	weaponed
vopns	weapons
vor	spring
vordaga	spring-days
vorn	our
vorra	ours
voru	was, were

Word List (Old Icelandic to English)

Old Icelandic English

Y, y

yður you, your, yours
yðvar you
yðvarn of-you
yfir over
yrði with

Word List *(English to Old Icelandic)*

English	Old Icelandic	English	Old Icelandic

A, a

English	Old Icelandic
a	að
a-black	svartan
a-blue	blán
about	Á, að, en, í, til, um
about-exchanged	umskipti
about-that-time	mund
abroad	utan
a-bull	griðung
accept	þiggir, þiggja
accepted	þiggja, þiggur
accomplished	Fær
according	því
accordingly	því
account-for	reifa
accusations	sökótt
across	þvers
advice	ráðlegast, ráðs
advisable	ráðlegast
advised	ráð
a-farm	bæ
a-friend	vinur
after	eftir, síðan
after-matter	eftirmáls
afterwards	eftir, Síðan, síðar
against	við
age	aldri
aggression	ágang
agreed	játtu
agreement	samið, stefna
a-haystack	heyvöndul
ahead	fyrir
a-house	hús
a-hurry	óðafári
a-journey	förum
a-little	lítinn
all	alla, alla, allan, allar, allir, allir, allri, alls, allt, allt, öll, öllu, öllum
all-great-man-like	allstórmannlega
allow	láta, ráða
all-prepared	albúnir
all-settle	alsáttir
all-well	allvel, allvel
alone	einn
along	eftir
also	og
am	er
a-man	maður, mann, manni
ambush	fyrirsát
a-meeting	fundur
am-named	heiti
a-month	mánuð
a-month's	mánaðar
an	eða
an-abundance	gnótt
an-axe	öxlina
and	eða, en, er, og
anew	nýju
an-idiot	mannfóli
another	aðra, annað, annað, annar, annar, annarri, öðru, öðrum
answer	svarið
answered	svarar
any	einum, neins, nokkura
any-longer	lengur
appears	líst
are	er, eru, eruð, séu
areas	sveitir
are-there	Eru
are-you	ertu
arms	fangi
Arnor (name)	Arnór, Arnóri
Arnor's (name)	Arnórs
arrange	ráðast
as	Á, að, er, sem, því
a-ship	skip
a-short-distance	skammt
as-if	sem
a-sign	marki
as-in-laws	mágsemdar
ask	beiðast
asked	bað, beiddi, spyr

Word List (English to Old Icelandic)

English	Old Icelandic
asked-for	heimti
asking	frétti
assembly	þing
assembly-man	þingmaður
assist	greiða
assistance	ásjá, ásjá, ásjár, liðsinni, liðveislu
as-soon-as	þegar
asunder	sundur
at	á, að, af, Í
at-home	heiman
attend	sótt
attended	sótt
attention	gaumur
away	brott
away-from	undan
awhile	hríð
axe	öxi

B, b

English	Old Icelandic
back	aftur, bak
back-from	úr
bad	illa
bad-temper	skapillur
bad-terms	illt
bald	sköllóttur
bank	bakkann
barely	varla
bathe	laug
battle	bardagi
be	Væri, værir, Ver, vera, verða
bear	ber, borið
bears	barist
became	lagði, urðu, varð, verða
because	því
because-of	fyrir
become	orðið, orðinn, verða, verði
becomes	vera, verður
bed-roll	húðfat
been	verið
before	áður, fyrir, fyrr, fyrri
before-us	fyrrum
began	hóf
begun	upphaf
behind	heldur
being	sé, séu, vera, verða
be-it	Vera
belt	belti
benefit	beini, gott
beside	hjá
best	best, besta, bestur
better	bæta, betra, betri, betur
between	meðal, milli
bid	boðið
Bjarni (name)	Bjarnar
black	blárri
boldly	djarflega, skörulega
Bollason (name)	Bollason, Bollasyni
Bolli (name)	Bolla, Bolli
Bolli's (name)	Bolla
both	báðir
bound	bindur, bundinn
bravely	drengilegsta
break	bregða
bring	færa
bringing	færa
broke	braut, bregður
broke-away	hvarf
broken	brotið
brother	bróðir, bróður
brothers	bræður
buckled	gyrður
bull	graðung, Graðungur
but	en, enn, er
by	við

C, c

English	Old Icelandic
called	heitaðist, kallaður
came	gengur, kemur, Kom, koma, komið, kominn, komu
cape	kápu
care	nenni
carried	borið

Word List (English to Old Icelandic)

English	Old Icelandic
case	*mál*
cast	*kasta*
cattle	*fé*
celebration	*fagnaði*
certainly	*víst, vísu*
challenge	*áskoran*
charged	*stefndi, stefnir*
charges	*atkvæðum*
chieftain	*höfðingi*
chieftains	*höfðingjar*
children	*börnum*
choosing	*kýstu*
chose	*kostur*
cloak	*skikkju*
close	*fast, nær*
closely	*fast*
closely-related	*náskyld*
clothing	*klæði*
coldly	*fálega*
collected	*safnar*
come	*kemur, kom, komið, kominn, komir, komnir, komum*
coming	*Kemur, koma, komnir*
companions	*förunautar, förunautar*
company	*sveit*
company-less	*liðfærri*
company-provided	*liðsafla*
compensate	*bæta*
compensation	*fébótum*
comrades	*félagar*
comradeship	*félagsskap*
concluded	*lauk*
consider	*þykir*
considerable	*ærin*
conversation	*talið*
convicted	*sekti*
conviction	*sakir*
costume	*búningur*
cowardly	*hann*
Crone's-Nose (name)	*kerlingarnef*
custom	*vanda*

D, d

English	Old Icelandic
Dagverdarnes (place)	*Dögurðarnes*
danger	*hættu*
dare	*þora*
dead	*dauður*
dearest	*dýrsta*
decide	*ráð, ráða, réði*
declare	*kalla, ráð*
deed-refuse	*nauðsynja*
defence	*varna*
defend	*verja*
deference	*tillæti*
describe	*lýsa*
deserve	*maklegt*
devastate	*eyða*
devilish-man	*skelmi*
did	*fór, gerði, gerðu*
difficulty	*erfið, vandi*
diminish	*minni*
discord	*sundurþykki*
discourage	*Letja*
discuss	*máli*
discussed	*ræddist*
dismounted	*Stigu*
dispute	*vandræði*
dissolved	*slitið*
dissuaded	*letjast*
district	*fjórðungi, héðra, héraði, héruð*
do	*gera, gerið, gerir*
doing	*gera, gerir*
done	*gert*
down	*aftur, leyst, niðri, niður, ofan*
drew	*bregður, dregur*
dwelled	*Dvöldust*

E, e

English	Old Icelandic
each	*hvert, hvorir*
eager	*kapp*
earlier	*áður*
earth	*jörð*

Word List (English to Old Icelandic)

English	Old Icelandic
earth-house	jarðhús
easily	hæglegt
eight	átta
eighteen	átján, átján
either-side	hvorirtveggju
ells	alna
encounter	finnast
encouraged	eggjar
endure	þola
equal	jafna
equal-many	jafnmarga
escape	sleppa
evening	kveldið
eventually	síðir
every	hverju
everyday	hversdaglega
evil	illu
exchange	skipta, tiltekju
exchanged	skipti, skiptust
expect	ætla, vænt, varði
expected	von

F, f

English	Old Icelandic
failed	fallið
fair	fögrum
fairly	haga
fallen	fallið, fallnir
falling	felldur
false	
falsehood	fólsku
famous-work	frægðarverk
far-away	fjarri
fared	farið
farm	bæ, búi
farmer	bóndi
farmhouse	bænum
fast	fast
fastened	fast
feast	veisla, veislu
fee	fá, fé
fell	fellur
few	fáir, fár, fátt
fiendship	fjandskap
fifteen	fimmtán

English	Old Icelandic
fight	berjast, berjist, víga
fight-the-case	vígsmálið
find	finna, finnum, Hitt
finished	lokið
floating	flaut
flock	flokk
follow	fylgja
followed	flýgur, Fylgir, fylgt
followers-many	fjölmenni
following-men	fjölmenna
follows	fylg, fylgi
foolish	afglapa
foolishly	fólið, heimsklega, heimsklegast
foolishness	heimskur
fool-of-yourself	undri
for	á, að, fyrir, í
forest-men	skógarmenn
forest-seeking	skóggangssök
for-me	mér
for-the-ambush	fyrirsátina
for-the-sake-of	sakir
fortunate	hamingja
fought	berjast
found	fann, fékk, fundust
frenzy-man	æðimaður
friend	vin, vinur
friendship	kærleikum, vinátta, vináttu, vinskap, vinskapar
friendship-matter	vinganarmál
from	á, að, af, af, frá, fram, úr, út
from-here	héðan
from-home	heiman
from-home-travel	heimanferð
from-out-of	úr
from-there	þaðan, þangað, þegar
full-of-people	fjölmennt
furious	óðast

G, g

English	Old Icelandic
Galmarstrond (place)	Galmarströnd
game	leik

Word List (English to Old Icelandic)

English	Old Icelandic
gave	*gaf, gáfu*
gets	*fengi*
gifts	*gjafar, gjafir, gjöfum*
give	*gefa, gefið*
given	*gefinn*
giving	*veita*
gladdest	*glaðasti*
go	*fara, ganga*
goes	*fer, fór*
going	*fara, ferð, ferðina, gangi*
gold-inlaid	*gullrekna*
gold-laid	*gulllagðan*
gold-ring	*fingurgull, gullhring, gullhringinn, gullhringur*
gone	*farið, farin, Gengið*
good	*góða, góðar, góðum, góður*
got	*fá, Fær, fékk, getið, getur*
grab	*grípa*
grant	*veita*
granted	*veitti*
great	*mikill, mikinn, miklir, Mjög*
greatly	*ágætlega, harðla*
great-man-like	*stórmannlegar*
great-man-ness	*stórmannlega*
greeted	*kvaddi*
greeting	*kveddi*
grew	*Óx*
grey	*grán*
grown	*vexti*
guarding	*verja*
Guddalir (place)	*Guðdölum*
Gudmund (name)	*Guðmundar, Guðmundur*
Gudrun (name)	*Guðrún*
guilt	*skyld*

H, h

English	Old Icelandic
had	*átt, átti, áttu, er, hafa, hafði, hafi, haft, hefir, hefur, höfðu, lætur, lagt, lét*
half	*hálfan, hvolfinu*
half-month's	*hálfs*
Hals (place)	*Háls, Hálsi*
hand	*hendi, hendur, hönd, höndum*
hardest	*harðasta, skarpasti*
harm	*mein*
has	*að, hafði, hefði, hefir, Höfum*
have	*að, áttir, eiga, ert, Haf, hafa, hafast, Hafið, hafir, haft, Hefi, hefir, höfum, leggja*
have-right	*heimul*
have-you	*áttu*
hay	*hey, heyjum*
hay-bundle	*heyvöndul*
hay-giving	*heygjöfinni*
haystacks	*andvirki*
hay-stacks	*heygarð*
he	*hana, hann, honum*
head	*höfuð*
healed	*greru*
heard	*heyrði, heyrir, heyrt*
Hegranes (place)-Assembly	*Hegranessþingi, Hegranessþings*
held	*hélt*
Helgi (name)	*Helga, Helgi*
Helgi's (name)	*Helga*
Heljardal Heath (place)	*Heljardalsheiði*
Hellu-Narfason (name)	*Hellu-Narfasonar*
Hellu-Narfi (name)	*Hellu-Narfa*
helmet	*hjálm*
her	*hana, henni, sér, síns*
herd	*hrossin*
here	*hér, hingað, þar*
hers	*hennar, sinn, sínum*
Hestanes (place)	*Hestanesi*

English	Old Icelandic
hey	*hey*
him	*hann, hans, honum, sér, sig, sín*
himself	*sér, sig*
his	*hann, hans, honum, sér, sín, sína, sinn, sinna, sinni, síns, sínu, sínum, sitt*
his-hands	*höndum*
Hjaltadal (place)	*Hjaltadal*
Hjaltasons (name)	*Hjaltasona, Hjaltasonu, Hjaltasynir*
Hjardarholt (place)	*Hjarðarholti*
Hof (place)	*Hofi, Hofs*
Hofdi (place)	*Höfða*
hold	*halda*
holds	*haldinn*
hollow	*holinu*
home	*heim, heima, þeim*
home-invitation	*heimboðanna*
home-invitations	*heimboðum*
homes	*alist*
home-sought	*heimsótt*
home-ways	*heimleiðis*
honour	*drengskap, frama, frama, framar, sæmd, sæmdar, sæmdarauki, sæmdir, sæmdum, virðið, virðing, virðingar, virðingu*
hooves	*klaufir*
horn	*horn*
horse	*hest, hesti*
horseback	*baki*
horses	*faraskjóta, hesta, hestana*
horse's	*hestsins*
hospitality	*varðveislu*
host	*bóndi*
housewife	*húsfreyja, húsfreyju*
how	*hversu, hvert, hvort*
how-so	*hversu*
Hrutafjord (place)	*Hrútafirði, Hrútafjarðar*
hundred	*hundruð*
hung	*hékk*
husband	*bónda*

I, i

English	Old Icelandic
I	*eg, mér*
ice	*ís*
if	*ef*
ill	*ill, illa, illt*
ill-advised	*ráðlaus*
ill-words	*illyrði*
immediately	*þegar*
impassable	*ófæru*
in	*á, að, eiga, en, í*
inconspicuous	*ófrýnlegur*
inhumane	*ómannlegt*
in-laws	*mágsemd*
in-sharing-together	*íhlutunarsamur*
inside	*inn, innan*
intend	*Ætla, ætlar*
intended	*Ætla, ætlað, ætlar*
into	*á, í, undir*
invited	*bauð, býður*
iron-shod	*járna*
is	*er, eru, í, sé, það*
it	*á, að, í, Það, þar, þetta*
it-is	*Er*
its	*til*

J, j

English	Old Icelandic
journey	*ferð, ferðir, leið*
joyfulness	*blíðu*

K, k

English	Old Icelandic
kill	*drepa, drepið*
killing	*drepið, víg*
king's-gift	*konungsnaut*
kinsman	*frænda, niður*
kinswoman	*frændkona, frændkonu*

Word List (English to Old Icelandic)

English	*Old Icelandic*	English	*Old Icelandic*
knife	*hníf*	man	*maður, manni*
know	*kunna, Veit, vita*	man-of-law	*málamaður*
Krossar (place)	*Krossa, Krossum*	many	*marga, margt, mjög, mörgu*
		many-men	*fjölmenna*

L, l

		Marbaeli (place)	*Marbæli, Marbælinga*
		marks	*merkur*
laid	*lagður*	marriage	*venslum*
land	*löndum*	married	*átti, gjaforð*
laughed	*brosti*	matter	*efni, mál, máli*
law	*lögum*	may	*má, mætti, máttu, mega, megi, megum*
law-man	*málamaður*		
lay	*leggið, leggja, liggur*	me	*mér, mig*
leapt	*hljóp*	meet	*fund, mæta, metast, móti, móts*
learned	*Frétti*		
leave	*láta*	meeting	*mót*
led	*létu*	men	*mann, manna, menn, mönnum*
Leg-Biter (name)	*Fótbít*		
less	*laus, minni*	merriest	*kátasti*
let	*látum, Lét, léti, Létu*	met	*finnast, fundust, hitti, hittust*
little	*lítið, lítill, lítils, litlu*	middle	*miðjan*
lived	*bjó, bjuggu*	might	*mætti*
Ljot (name)	*Ljóti, Ljótur*	Miklabaer (place)	*Miklabæ*
Ljot (place)	*Ljóti, Ljóts*	mine	*mér, mig, mín, mína, minn, minna, mínum, mitt*
Ljot's (name)	*Ljóts*		
loath	*leiða*		
lodging	*vistar*	misguided	*ófallið*
long	*lengi*	mockery	*hæðileg*
longer	*lengri*	Modruvellir (place)	*Möðruvöllu*
look	*leita, líta*	mood	*skapi*
looked	*litu*	more	*fleiri, meir, meira*
looks	*horfist*	morning	*morguninn*
loss	*sviptir*	most	*mest, mesta, mestum*
lot	*hlut*	mother's-sister's-son	*systrungur*
lowly-deed	*níðingsverk*	mourned	*harmaði*
luck	*hamingja, heill*	much	*margt, mig, mikið, mikill, mikilli, mikinn, mikla, miklu, miklum, mjög*
luck-promised	*giftuvænlegur*		
lunged	*lagði, leggur*		
		my	*mig, Mín, mína, mínum*

M, m

made	*ger, gerð, gerði, gerðu, gert*

N, n

make	*fallið, gerðinni*		
make-friends	*vingast*	name	*nafn, nafn*
		named	*heitinn, heitir, hét*

Word List (English to Old Icelandic)

English	*Old Icelandic*	English	*Old Icelandic*
Narfason (name)	*Narfason*	on	*á, í*
nature	*skaplyndi*	one	*eina, einn, einnhvern*
near	*nær, undir*	one-agreement	*einsætt*
nearest	*næst*	only	*einir, einn*
near-to	*nálega*	open-whole	*vinhollir*
necessity	*nauðsyn*	opposite	*hvorir*
need	*Þarf, þurfa, þurfi*	or	*eða*
need-you	*þarftu*	ordered	*bað*
negatively	*þungt*	other	*annað, öðrum*
neither	*hvergi*	other-knowing	*öðruvís*
never	*aldrei*	others	*aðrir, öðru, öðrum*
new	*nýjum*	Ottar (name)	*Óttar, Óttari*
news	*frétt, tíðinda*	our	*okkars, vér, vorn*
nights	*nætur*	ours	*oss, vorra*
no	*eigi, ekki, engi, engrar*	out	*út*
noble	*skörungur*	outlawed	*sektan*
noblest	*göfgustu*	outlawry	*skóggang*
none	*eigi, enga, engi, engis, engrar, öngvir*	out-of	*úr*
nor	*en*	outside	*úti*
north	*norðan, norður*	over	*yfir*
northerners	*Norðlendingum*	overcome	*Barst*
not	*eigi, ekki*	own	*eign, eigna*
nothing	*ekki, engu*		
now	*nú*		

O, o

P, p

English	*Old Icelandic*
obtain	*ná, seilast*
occurrence	*tilfelli*
of	*á, að, af, af, úr*
of-all	*allra*
off	*af*
of-family-small	*ættsmár*
offer	*beiða, biðja, bjóða*
offered	*boðið*
of-silver	*silfurs*
often	*Oft*
of-them	*þeirra*
of-they	*þeirra*
of-violent-language	*málóði*
of-wealth	*fjár*
of-you	*yðvarn*
Olaf (name)	*Ólafi, Ólafur*
Olaf's (name)	*Ólafs*
parted	*skilnaði*
parting	*skilnaði*
passed	*leið, líður*
pay	*aura, gjalda*
peace	*kyrrt*
peaceful	*fríð*
Peacock (name)	*pá*
people	*menn, mönnum*
people's	*manna*
person	*manninn*
place	*stað*
plans	*ætlað*
pledged	*Hét*
plenty-of	*ærið*
plotting	*fjörráð*
plotting-against	*fjörráð*
poleaxe	*refði*
poorly	*fálega*
popular	*vinsæll*
possible	*hægt*

Word List (English to Old Icelandic)

English	*Old Icelandic*	English	*Old Icelandic*
postpone	*fresta*	ridden	*riðið*
powerful	*ríki*	ride	*ríð, ríða, riðið, ríðið*
Powerful (name)	*ríka*	riding	*ráðinn, reið*
prepare	*búast*	right	*réttindum*
prepared	*bjóst, búið, búin, býr, býst*	right-knowing	*réttvísi*
		risk	*voða*
preparing	*búnir*	river	*ána*
prevent	*skirra*	rocks	*grjóti*
pride	*metnaður*	rode	*ræðst, Réðst, Reið, Ríða, riðu, ríður*
promised	*hét*		
promising	*efnilegastur*	running	*hlaupi*
protect	*verja*		
provinces	*héruðum*		

Q, q

quickly	*skjótt, snarlega*

R, r

rampages	*ofríki*
ran	*Hleypa, hleypur, hljóp, hljópu*
rather	*heldur, helst*
realised	*þykjast*
recoiled	*hrökkva*
reconcile	*sættast*
rectify	*leiðréttu*
refuse	*níta*
reins	*tauma*
releasing	*leystur*
relieved	*fegin, létti, léttu*
renowned	*ágætir*
repay	*selja*
reported	*Fréttist, Fréttust, títt*
resolved	*greiddist*
respect	*virðing*
respect-kindly	*virðingarvænlegt*
rest	*æja*
return	*aftur, móti, ömbun, snúa*
returned	*aftur*
Reykir (place)	*Reykja*
rich	*auðigur*

S, s

safe	*fritt, heilir*
saga	*sögu*
sagas	*sögum*
said	*kvað, lést, sagði, sagði, sagt, segir, svarar, tala*
sake	*sakir*
same	*sömu*
sat	*Sat, Sátu*
saw	*leit, Sá, sáu, sér, sjá*
say	*segi, segja, tel*
scathed	*skaða*
see	*Sé*
seeing	*sjáandi*
seek	*leita, leitast, sækir*
seemed	*sýna, Sýnist*
seems	*þætti, þykir*
self-judgement	*dóm, sjálfdæmi*
send	*sendi*
separate	*skilja*
separated	*skildi, skildist, Skildu, Skildust, skilið, skilja*
serves	*gegnir*
set	*sett, settist, Setur*
set-out	*fer*
settle	*sætt*
settlers	*búa*
seven	*sjö*
several	*nokkura*
shall	*Mun, munu, Munuð, munum, skal, skalt, skaltu, skuli, Skulu*

Word List (English to Old Icelandic)

English	Old Icelandic
shall-be	skal
shall-you	muntu, skaltu
she	hún
shield	skildi, skjöld
shields	skildir
shining	blika
ships	skips
short-distance	skammt
shot	skýtur
should	mun, mundi, muni, munt, Munu, Munum, skal, skuluð, skulum, skyldi, skyldu
should-you	Muntu
show	lýsa, sýna
showed	sýnir
shown	lýst, sýnt
side	hlið
sides	megin
Sigrid (name)	Sigríðar, Sigríði, Sigríður
since	En, því
sit	sitja
sit-in-ambush	sæta, sitja
sitting	sátu, setuefni, sitja
Skagafjord (place)	Skagafirði, Skagafjarðar
Skeid (place)	Skeið, Skeiði
skin-cloak	skinnstakki
slander	illmæli
slanderous	óorðan
slanderous-men	öfundarmenn
slaying-of	víg
smaller	smærri
snag-cornered	snaghyrnda
snow	snjór
so	nú, sá, sé, svo, það
solved	leyst
some	nokkuð, nokkurir
something	nokkuð
somewhat	nokkuð, nokkur, nokkura
son	Son, sonar, sonur
son-of	son
Son-of-Bolli (name)	Bollason
Son-of-Thord (name)	Þórðarsonar
Sons-of-Hjalti (name)	Hjaltasynir
son-yours	sveinsins
sought	sótt, sótti
south	suður
spare	spara
speak	máli, tala
speaking	mælti
speak-to	mál
spear	spjót, spjóti, spjótið, spjótinu
spoke	kvað, mælti, mæltu, Tala
sport	leika, leikum
sprang	spretta
spring	vor
spring-days	vordaga
spurred	keyrði, keyrir
standing	staddur
Starri (name)	Starri
Starri-of-Guddalir	Guðdala-Starra
startled	brá
Stately-man (name)	stærimaður, stærimann, stærimanni, stertimaður
stay	setið
stayed	sat, sátu, setjast, Situr
steal	stela
stealing	stela
step	stíga
still	kyrrt
stolen	stolið
stood	standanda, stóð, studdist
stop	hættu
strength	styrk
striking	höggur
such	sig, slík, því
summer	sumar, sumarið
summoned	stefndi, stefnu
summons	stefnu
suspect	grunur
suspected	grunaði
Svarfadardal (place)	Svarfaðardal, Svarfaðardals, Svarfaðardalsár, Svarfdæla

Word List (English to Old Icelandic)

English	*Old Icelandic*

T, t

English	*Old Icelandic*
take	tæki, Tak, taka, takir
taken	taka, tekið, tekist
talked	mælt, töluðu
talking	tal
team-minded	liðsinnaður
tearing	rífa
ten	tigi
test	freista, reyndu
tested	reyna
than	en
thanked	kvað, þakkaði, þakkar
thanks	Þakka, þakkar, þökk
that	að, en, er, í, sem, það, Þetta, því
the	á, að, enn, er, hið, hin, Hina, hinn, hins, hinu, hinum, í, Þá, þann, Þeir
the-after-matter	eftirmálinu
the-assembly	alþingi, þing, þingið, þinginu, þingsins
the-battle	bardagann
the-booth	búðina
the-booth-doors	búðardyrunum
the-boy	sveininn
the-brothers	bræðra
the-bull	boli, graðungurinn
the-captain	stýrimann
the-case	málið, málinu
the-charges	sakir
the-compound	virkið
the-district	sveitum
the-earth	jörð
the-emperor	stólkonungurinn
the-farm	bæinn, bænum, bú
the-farmer	bónda, bóndi
the-feast	veisla
the-fields	velli
theft	þjófnað
the-gift	gjafir
the-gifts	gjafirnar
the-hay	desjarnar, heyinu

English	*Old Icelandic*
the-heath	heiðina
the-horses	hestana
the-ice	ísinn
their	sína, þeirra
theirs	sína, sinn, sinna, sínum, þeirra
the-journey	ferðinni
the-killing-of	víg
the-leg	fæti
them	sér, þeim, þeirra
the-man	maðurinn, mannsins
the-matter	efni, mál, máli, málið, málum
the-middle	miðri
the-more	meiri
themselves	sér
then	en, enn, er, síðan, þá, þann, þegar, Þeir, Var
the-night	nóttina
the-northerners	Norðlendinga
the-pastures	afréttum
there	eru, þangað, Þangað, þar, þar, Þeir
therefore	því
the-ring	hringinn
the-river	áin, ána, ána, ánni, ár, árinnar
the-same	saman
these	hina, þessar, þessir
the-shield	skildinum, Skjöldurinn
the-slaying	vígi
the-slaying-of	víg
the-slope	hlíðinni
the-son-of	sonur
the-spear	spjótið
the-struggle	Sóknin
the-summons	stefnuna, stefnunni
the-sword	sverðinu
the-truest	sannast
the-unseen-man	launmaðurinn
the-way	leiðina
the-wind	vindur
the-worst	verst
the-worth	verð
the-wounds	Sárum
they	sínum, þá, Þau, Þau, þeim, Þeir, þeirra

132

Word List (English to Old Icelandic)

English	*Old Icelandic*	English	*Old Icelandic*
they-of	þeirra	to-people	mönnum
thieves	þjófarnir	to-ride	ríða
things	hlutir	to-say	segja
think	hugði, hugðum, hygg, hyggja, Þykir, þykist, þykjast	to-them	þeim
		to-travel	fara
		to-you	þér
this	í, sé, sín, sitt, það, þenna, þess, þessa, þessi, þessu, Þetta	trading-men	kaupmenn, kaupmönnum
		travel	færi, fara, farið, ferð, ferðar, ferðinni
Thord (name)	Þórð, Þórðar, Þórði, Þórður	travelled	fær, farið, Fer, fór, Fóru
Thordis (name)	Þórdís		
Thorgrim (name)	Þorgrímur	travelled-you	fórstu
Thorolf (name)	Þórólf, Þórólfi, Þórólfur	travelling	farinn, ferð
		travels	fer
Thorolf's (name)	Þórólfs	treacherous	fláráðum
Thorstein (name)	Þorstein, Þorstein, Þorsteini, Þorsteinn	treachery	brekráð
		treasures	gripirnir
Thorstein's (name)	Þorsteini, Þorsteins	trim	kvisti
Thorvald (name)	Þorvaldi, Þorvaldi, Þorvaldur	trouble	vandræðum
		true	
though	þó, þótt	true	
thought	hugðu, hugsar, þótti, þóttu, þykir	truly	sannast
		trust	trausts
threat	hót	try	freista
three	þriggja, þrír, þrjá, þrjár	trying	reyna
through	gegnum	Tunga (place)	Tungu
Thufur (place)	Þúfum	tunic	kyrtil
Thvera (place)	Þverá, Þverár	turf-stacks	torfstakka
time	tíma	turn	horfa, hverfa, hverfið, snúa
to	á, að, áðu, af, ást, í, það, til, við		
		turned	hallaði, Sneri, snerist
to-accept	þiggja	twelve	tólf
to-do	gera	twice	tvenn
to-expect	von	two	tvo
together	jafnsaman, saman, saman		
to-give	gefa		
to-going	atgöngu		
to-have	eiga, hafa		

U, u

English	*Old Icelandic*
to-him	honum
to-invite	bjóða
told	sagði, sagði, sagt, segir, töluðu
to-me	mér
took	tækist, tekur, tók, tókst
took-to	tóku

English	*Old Icelandic*
unanimously	einhlítt
uncertain	óvíst
understanding	skiljum
un-equal-men	ójafnaðarmenn
un-faring	ófarin
unfriendly	óvinveittur
un-friends	óvinum

Word List (English to Old Icelandic)

English	*Old Icelandic*	English	*Old Icelandic*
un-good	*ómæt*	well	*féllu, vel*
unholy	*óheilagur*	well-willing	*vel*
unmanageable	*ofstýri*	went	*fór, Fóru, ganga, gekk, gengu, gengur*
unqualified	*óhæfu*	were	*er, eru, Var, vera, voru*
un-right-knowing	*óréttvís*		
un-rule	*ofríki*	west	*vestur*
unruliness	*róstum*	what	*en, hvað, hvar, Hverja, hvern, hvert*
unruly	*ofríki*		
un-substantial-company	*óliðdrjúgur*	when	*er, Nær, þá, Þegar*
		where	*hvar, varstu*
unsuitable	*óliðlegt*	whether	*en, hvort*
until	*til*	which	*er, Hvert, sem*
up	*á, upp, uppi*	while	*stund*
upped	*upp*	white	*hvítur*
up-saying	*uppsögn*	who	*er, hver, Hverjir, sem*
Urdskriduholar (place)	*Urðskriðuhóla*	wife	*kona, konu*
us	*okkur, oss*	wife-of	*kona*
usually	*jafnan*	wild	*ólman*
		will	*vil, vilja, Viljum*

V, v

		willing	*vildi, vilja, viljaður*
vagrancy	*verðgang*	winter	*veturinn*
value	*virða*	winters	*vetra*
Vellir (place)	*Völlu, Völlum*	wisdom	*spekt*
visit	*vitja*	wish	*vil, Vildi, vilja, vilji, viljir, vilt*

W, w

		wished	*vildi, vill*
		wishing	*vill*
wait	*bíður*	with	*á, með, um, við, yrði*
ward-knowing	*varðveita*	with-fleetness	*flytjir*
warranted	*varða*	with-taken	*viðtökur*
warriors	*kappi*	with-taking	*viðtökur*
was	*á, en, er, sé, væri, var, varð, voru*	wit-less	*vitlaus*
		word	*orði*
was-named	*hét*	words	*orð, orða, orðið*
way	*leið, veg, vegar*	work	*verk*
way-out	*færi*	worse	*versna*
we	*vér*	worth	*verðugt, verður, virða, virðing*
wealth	*fé, fjár*		
weaponed	*vopnaðir*	worthiness	*virðing*
weapons	*vopn, vopns*	worthy	*göfugt, vert*
weathered	*veður*	would	*mun, mundi, mundu, muni, munu*
we-get	*hljótum*		
welcomed	*fagnað*	would-be	*munu, værir, verða*
		wound	*sár*
		wounded	*Meiddi, sár*
		wounding	*sár*

Word List (English to Old Icelandic)

English	*Old Icelandic*
wounds	*sár, sára*
wretch	*vesalmenni*

Y, y

you	*þér, þið, þig, þinn, þú, yður, yðvar*
young	*ungur*
your	*þér, yður*
yours	*þína, þinn, þinnar, þinni, þitt, yður*
yourself	*sjálfan*
you-two	*þið*
Yule (name)	*jól*

A Word Comparison of Old Norse and Old Icelandic Words

Old Norse	Old Icelandic	English	Old Norse	Old Icelandic	English
á	af	at	barizt	barist	bears
á	af	of	berist	berjist	fight
áðr	áður	before	berr	ber	bear
áðr	áður	earlier	betr	betur	better
æðimaðr	æðimaður	frenzy-man	bezt	best	best
ærit	ærið	plenty-of	bezta	besta	best
ætlat	ætlað	intended	beztr	bestur	best
ætlat	ætlað	plans	bíðr	bíður	wait
aftr	aftur	back	bindr	bindur	bound
aftr	aftur	down	blári	blárri	black
aftr	aftur	return	boðit	boðið	bid
aftr	aftur	returned	boðit	boðið	offered
ágætliga	ágætlega	greatly	borit	borið	bear
aldri	aldrei	never	borit	borið	carried
alizt	alist	homes	bræðr	bræður	brothers
allstórmannliga	allstórmannlega	all-great-man-like	bregðr	bregður	broke
			bregðr	bregður	drew
annarr	annar	another	brotit	brotið	broken
annat	annað	another	búðardurunum	búðardyrunum	the-booth-doors
annat	annað	other			
Arnórr	Arnór	Arnor (name)	búit	búið	prepared
ásjá	ásjár	assistance	búningr	búningur	costume
áskorun	áskoran	challenge	býðr	býður	invited
at	að	a	dauðr	dauður	dead
at	að	about	djarfliga	djarflega	boldly
at	að	as	dregr	dregur	drew
at	að	at	drengiligsta	drengilegsta	bravely
at	að	for	drepit	drepið	kill
at	að	from	drepit	drepið	killing
at	að	has	dvölðust	Dvöldust	dwelled
at	að	have	efniligastr	efnilegastur	promising
at	að	in	einhvern	einnhvern	one
at	að	it	ek	eg	I
at	að	of	em	er	am
at	að	that	engir	öngvir	none
at	að	the	erfit	erfið	difficulty
at	að	to	fagnat	fagnað	welcomed
átzt	ást	to	fáliga	fálega	coldly
auðigr	auðigur	rich	fáliga	fálega	poorly

A Word Comparison of Old Norse and Old Icelandic

Old Norse	Old Icelandic	English	Old Norse	Old Icelandic	English
fallit	fallið	failed	gyrðr	gyrður	buckled
fallit	fallið	fallen	hæðilig	hæðileg	mockery
fallit	fallið	make	hægligt	hæglegt	easily
fararskjóta	faraskjóta	horses	hálfsmánaðar	hálfs	half-month's
farit	farið	fared	heðan	héðan	from-here
farit	farið	gone	heðra	héðra	district
farit	farið	travelled	hefr	hefur	had
fekk	fékk	found	heimskliga	heimsklega	foolishly
fekk	fékk	got	heimskligast	heimsklegast	foolishly
felldr	felldur	falling	heimskr	heimskur	foolishness
fellr	fellur	fell	hekk	hékk	hung
fellu	féllu	well	heldr	heldur	behind
ferr	fer	goes	heldr	heldur	rather
ferr	fer	set-out	helt	hélt	held
ferr	Fer	travelled	helzt	helst	rather
ferr	fer	travels	hendr	hendur	hand
ferr	ferð	going	heraði	héraði	district
ferr	ferð	travel	heruð	héruð	district
fingrgull	fingurgull	gold-ring	heruðum	héruðum	provinces
finnim	finnum	find	hingat	hingað	here
flýgr	flýgur	followed	hittir	hitti	met
flytir	flytjir	with-fleetness	hleypr	hleypur	ran
fólit	fólið	foolishly	hliðhollir	vinhollir	open-whole
fórtu	fórstu	travelled-you	höggr	höggur	striking
fundr	fundur	a-meeting	hon	hún	she
gaumr	gaumur	attention	hugða	hugði	think
gengit	Gengið	gone	hválfinu	hvolfinu	half
gengr	gengur	came	hvárir	hvorir	each
gengr	gengur	went	hvárir	hvorir	opposite
getit	getið	got	hvárirtveggju	hvorirtveggju	either-side
getr	getur	got	hvárt	hvort	how
giftuvænligr	giftuvænlegur	luck-promised	hvárt	hvort	whether
gjafar	gjafir	gifts	hvat	hvað	what
gjafar	gjafir	the-gift	hverir	Hverjir	who
gjafarnar	gjafirnar	the-gifts	hverr	hver	who
góðr	góður	good	hversdagliga	hversdaglega	everyday
graðung	griðung	a-bull	hvítr	hvítur	white
graðungr	Graðungur	bull	íhann	hann	cowardly
graðungrinn	graðungurinn	the-bull	íhlutunarsamr	íhlutunarsamur	in-sharing-together
grunr	grunur	suspect	in	hin	the
Guðmundr	Guðmundur	Gudmund (name)	ina	Hina	the
gullhringr	gullhringur	gold-ring	ina	hina	these

A Word Comparison of Old Norse and Old Icelandic

Old Norse	Old Icelandic	English	Old Norse	Old Icelandic	English
inn	hinn	the	málamaðr	málamaður	law-man
ins	hins	the	málamaðr	málamaður	man-of-law
inum	hinum	the	málit	málið	the-case
íss	ís	ice	málit	málið	the-matter
it	hið	the	með	við	with
kærleik	kærleikum	friendship	merkr	merkur	marks
kallaðr	kallaður	called	metnaðr	metnaður	pride
kemr	kemur	came	mik	mig	me
kemr	kemur	come	mik	mig	mine
kemr	Kemur	coming	mik	mig	much
kníf	hníf	knife	mik	mig	my
komim	komum	come	mikit	mikið	much
komit	komið	came	mjök	Mjög	great
komit	komið	come	mjök	mjög	many
kómu	komu	came	mjök	mjög	much
kostr	kostur	chose	morgininn	morguninn	morning
kveldit	kveldið	evening	muna	muni	should
kvista	kvisti	trim	mynda	mundi	should
lætr	lætur	had	myndi	mundi	should
lagðr	lagður	laid	myndi	mundi	would
launmaðrinn	launmaðurinn	the-unseen-man	myndi	mundu	would
			nætr	nætur	nights
leggr	leggur	lunged	náliga	nálega	near-to
leikim	leikum	sport	ne	en	nor
lengr	lengur	any-longer	niðr	niður	down
leystr	leystur	releasing	niðr	niður	kinsman
lézt	lést	said	nökkura	nokkura	any
liðfæri	liðfærri	company-less	nökkura	nokkura	several
líðr	líður	passed	nökkura	nokkura	somewhat
liðsinnaðr	liðsinnaður	team-minded	nökkurir	nokkurir	some
liðveizlu	liðveislu	assistance	nökkurr	nokkur	somewhat
liggr	liggur	lay	nökkut	nokkuð	some
lítit	lítið	little	nökkut	nokkuð	something
lízt	líst	appears	nökkut	nokkuð	somewhat
Ljótr	Ljótur	Ljot (name)	norðr	norður	north
lokit	lokið	finished	ófallit	ófallið	misguided
maðr	maður	a-man	ófrýnligr	ófrýnlegur	inconspicuous
maðr	maður	man			
maðrinn	maðurinn	the-man	óheilagr	óheilagur	unholy
mætta	mætti	might	ok	og	also
mágsemð	mágsemd	in-laws	ok	og	and
mágsemðar	mágsemdar	as-in-laws	okkr	okkur	us
makligt	maklegt	deserve	Óláfi	Ólafi	Olaf (name)

A Word Comparison of Old Norse and Old Icelandic

Old Norse	Old Icelandic	English
Óláfr	Ólafur	Olaf (name)
Óláfs	Ólafs	Olaf's (name)
óliðdrjúgr	óliðdrjúgur	un-substantial-company
óliðligt	óliðlegt	unsuitable
ómannligt	ómannlegt	inhumane
ombun	ömbun	return
ór	úr	back-from
ór	úr	from
ór	úr	from-out-of
ór	úr	of
ór	úr	out-of
orðit	orðið	become
orðit	orðið	words
óréttvíss	óréttvís	un-right-knowing
Óttarr	Óttar	Ottar (name)
óvinveittr	óvinveittur	unfriendly
ráðlauss	ráðlaus	ill-advised
ráðligast	ráðlegast	advice
ráðligast	ráðlegast	advisable
réða	réði	decide
réttendum	réttindum	right
reyndi	reyndu	test
riðinn	ráðinn	riding
riðit	riðið	ridden
riðit	riðið	ride
ríðr	ríður	rode
sá	sáu	saw
sæmð	sæmd	honour
sæmðar	sæmdar	honour
sæmðarauki	sæmdarauki	honour
sæmðir	sæmdir	honour
sæmðum	sæmdum	honour
sakar	sakir	conviction
sakar	sakir	for-the-sake-of
sakar	sakir	for-the-sake-of
sakar	sakir	sake
sakar	sakir	the-charges
samit	samið	agreement
sárr	sár	wounded
sé	séu	are
sé	séu	being
segir	svarar	said
sekðan	sektan	outlawed
sekði	sekti	convicted
setit	setið	stay
setr	Setur	set
Sigríðr	Sigríður	Sigrid (name)
sik	sig	him
sik	sig	himself
sik	sig	such
silfrs	silfurs	of-silver
sitr	Situr	stayed
sjándi	sjáandi	seeing
sjau	sjö	seven
skapillr	skapillur	bad-temper
skilði	skildi	separated
skilðist	skildist	separated
skilðu	Skildu	separated
skilðust	Skildust	separated
skilit	skilið	separated
skjöldrinn	Skjöldurinn	the-shield
sköllóttr	sköllóttur	bald
sköruliga	skörulega	boldly
skörungr	skörungur	noble
skylda	skyldi	should
skyli	skuli	shall
skýtr	skýtur	shot
slitit	slitið	dissolved
smæri	smærri	smaller
snarliga	snarlega	quickly
sonr	Son	son
sonr	son	son-of
sonr	sonur	son
sonr	sonur	the-son-of
spekð	spekt	wisdom
spjótit	spjótið	spear
spjótit	spjótið	the-spear
spyrr	spyr	asked
staddr	staddur	standing
Stærimaðr	stærimaður	Stately-man (name)

A Word Comparison of Old Norse and Old Icelandic

Old Norse	Old Icelandic	English	Old Norse	Old Icelandic	English
Stertimaðr	stertimaður	Stately-man (name)	Þórðr	Þórður	Thord (name)
stolit	stolið	stolen	Þorgrímr	Þorgrímur	Thorgrim (name)
stólkonungrinn	stólkonungurinn	the-emperor	Þórólfr	Þórólfur	Thorolf (name)
stórmannliga	stórmannlega	great-man-ness	Þorvaldr	Þorvaldur	Thorvald (name)
stórmannligar	stórmannlegar	great-man-like	þrír	þrjá	three
suðr	suður	south	þykkir	þykir	consider
sumarit	sumarið	summer	þykkir	þykir	seems
sundr	sundur	asunder	þykkir	Þykir	think
sundrþykki	sundurþykki	discord	þykkir	þykir	thought
svá	nú	so	þykkist	þykist	think
svá	svo	so	þykkjast	þykjast	realised
systrungr	systrungur	mother's-sister's-son conversation	þykkjast	þykjast	think
talit	talið	taken	þykkjumst	Þykist	think
tekit	tekið	taken	tíðenda	tíðinda	news
tekizt	tekist	taken	tigu	tigi	ten
tekr	tekur	took	tvá	tvo	two
þangat	þangað	from-there	ungr	ungur	young
þangat	þangað	there	útan	utan	abroad
þat	það	is	váða	voða	risk
þat	Það	it	væra	Væri	be
þat	það	so	ván	von	expected
þat	það	that	ván	von	to-expect
þat	það	this	vanða	vanda	custom
þat	það	to	vápn	vopn	weapons
þat	þetta	it	vápnaðir	vopnaðir	weaponed
þeir	þá	they	vápns	vopns	weapons
þeira	þeirra	of-them	vár	vor	spring
þeira	þeirra	of-they	várdaga	vordaga	spring-days
þeira	þeirra	their	varðveizlu	varðveislu	hospitality
þeira	þeirra	theirs	várn	vorn	our
þeira	þeirra	them	várra	vorra	ours
þeira	þeirra	they	vartu	varstu	where
þeira	þeirra	they-of	váru	voru	was
þiggr	þiggur	accepted	váru	voru	were
þik	þig	you	veðr	veður	weathered
þingit	þingið	the-assembly	veizla	veisla	feast
þingmaðr	þingmaður	assembly-man	veizla	veisla	the-feast
þit	þið	you	veizlu	veislu	feast
þit	þið	you-two	velviljaðr	vel	well-willing
			venzlum	venslum	marriage
			verðr	verður	becomes

A Word Comparison of Old Norse and Old Icelandic

Old Norse	Old Icelandic	English
verðr	verður	worth
verit	verið	been
vestr	vestur	west
vetrinn	veturinn	winter
vígsmálit	vígsmálið	fight-the-case
vilda	Vildi	wish
vilir	viljir	wish
vilja	vilji	wish
vill	vilt	wish
vindr	vindur	the-wind
vinr	vinur	a-friend
vinr	vinur	friend
virðingarvænligt	virðingarvænlegt	respect-kindly
virkit	virkið	the-compound
vitlauss	vitlaus	wit-less
yðr	yður	you
yðr	yður	your